Low-Glycemic Meals in Minutes
Re-set Your Life with Healthy Eating and Active Living

Contents

Foreword *by Ray D. Strand, M.D.*		3
Introduction		5
Success Stories		7
Healthy Eating 101		9
About the Book's Recipes		11
Quick Prep		12
Quick Prep Recipes	Nutrition Shakes	17
	Quick Breakfast Ideas	20
	Poultry	23
	Ground Meat	27
	Fish	31
	Mix and Match Wraps and Pitas	34
	"Clean Sweep" Leftovers	35
	Salsas, Spreads and Dips	37
30 Minute Solutions	Brunch	41
	Soups	48
	Salads and Dressings	55
	Main Meals	73
	Meatless Meals and Side Dishes	79
	Desserts	95
	Snack Ideas	99
Menu Planning	Overview	105
	One-week Sample Menu, Phase 1	106
	One-week Sample Menu, Phase 2	107
The Importance of Cellular Nutrition		109
Move It and Lose It!		111
Shopping List		114
Index		116
Acknowledgements		120

Foreword

Today we are in the midst of the greatest health care crisis to hit the modern western world—obesity. What is even more concerning is the fact that it is now projected that over 30% of the next generation will develop diabetes sometime in their life. In this world of unparalleled medical information, many of us are dying and suffering needlessly because of lack of knowledge. How we choose to live our lives is a major factor in determining not only the length of our lives, but also our quality of life.

The most important aspect of our health is determined by the foods we choose to eat. It is becoming more and more obvious that the highly processed foods we are consuming today are one of the main reasons we are facing the obesity and diabetes epidemics. Learning to prepare and serve meals that contain good, low-glycemic carbohydrates along with good fats and proteins, is key to your health and the health of your family. When you combine a healthy diet with a modest exercise program and high quality nutritional supplements, you give yourself the absolute best chance of protecting your health and maintaining a healthy weight.

There are times when a book comes along that will greatly impact many lives. This book by Laura Kalina and Cheryl Christian is one of those books. The principles used to create the wonderful recipes found in this book are based on health concepts I presented in my book, *Healthy for Life* (Real Life Press 2005). Dr. David Jenkins, a professor at the University of Toronto, fearlessly challenged the long-held concept of simple sugars versus complex carbohydrates as the way to determine how quickly our blood sugar rises following the intake of carbohydrates.

In 1981, Dr. David Jenkins released a study where he compared blood sugar levels following the ingestion of a particular carbohydrate to those following the ingestion of a control food (glucose). From the resulting differences in blood sugar levels emerged the concept of the "glycemic index." He gave glucose a glycemic index of 100 and all other foods tested were indexed based on how much they raised blood sugar. His findings shocked the medical community. He found that complex carbohydrates like bread, rice, cereals, and potatoes actually spiked our blood sugar much faster than table sugar.

Studies have revealed that 85 to 90 percent of the carbohydrates that adults and children are eating today in the U.S. and Canada are highly processed and high-glycemic. This has led us to repeatedly spike our blood sugar and eventually become much less sensitive to our own insulin. The insulin resistance that has developed because of our poor diet and lack of physical activity is the primary reason we are in the midst of not only an obesity epidemic, it is the major reason so many of us are becoming diabetic. It has now been shown that nearly 25 percent of the adult population has full-blown insulin resistance and another 25 percent are well on their way of developing it. This leads to a constellation of health problems that has been defined by the medical community as the "metabolic syndrome." These individuals develop high blood pressure, abnormal lipids, increased blood clotting, significant weight gain, and are at high risk of developing heart disease and diabetes. When this occurs, you not only begin aging much faster than you should, but you also gain an unusual amount of weight around your middle that you just can't lose. You begin to hold on to fat like a sponge holds on to water. This is all the result of an underlying resistance to your own insulin.

This cutting edge book provides you and your family with the guidance necessary to begin eating healthy low-glycemic carbohydrates like whole, fresh fruits and vegetables along with whole grains. The Phase 1 recipes allow you to not only break the damaging cycle of spiking blood sugar, but also allow you to have victory over your cravings and emotional eating. Over time, you actually become more and more sensitive to your own insulin again. When you combine healthy, low-glycemic carbohydrates with good fats and proteins, you allow your body the best opportunity to become more sensitive to your own insulin. This is especially true when you combine this healthy diet with a modest exercise program and high quality nutritional supplementation. Once you have successfully reached your weight and health goals, you are able to move on to Phase 2 of the *Healthy for Life Program*, which reintroduces healthy grains, potatoes, and cereals.

It is important to point out the fact that some of you are now gaining a fear of consuming carbohydrates because of the low- or no-carbohydrate diets that are permeating the book shelves. You must realize that our bodies need and desire good carbohydrates, which also contain all of those great vitamins, minerals, and antioxidants that our bodies need and require. Simply eating 8 to 12 servings daily of fruits and vegetables will decrease your risk of heart disease, stroke, diabetes, cancer, and Alzheimer's disease by two- to three-fold.

Laura and Cheryl make these recommendations so easy and obtainable. You now have a great resource of easy-to-prepare, healthy recipes that provide those good carbohydrates, good fats, and good protein. The food we consume is one of the greatest drugs we put into our body. Take the time to learn how to prepare these healthy, delicious recipes that will help reverse any carbohydrate cravings you may have and at the same time protect your health.

I think you will find that these innovative recipes not only taste great, they are also easy to prepare. Your family will enjoy the pleasure of sharing these meals together as everyone's health improves. Diets simply do not work. We need to learn how to prepare and eat healthy delicious food all over again. This book will make your task so much easier and so much more fun.

Ray D. Strand, M.D.

Introduction

Congratulations, you have taken the next step towards a healthier you! Drawing from their extensive background, Cheryl Christian and Laura Kalina have come together to share their innovative, real-life-tested and family-approved formulas to ease you into a healthy lifestyle.

Cheryl Christian, as a Certified Personal Trainer, understands the need for families and individuals of all ages to make healthier choices when it comes to meal planning. As a busy mother of two boys, she also understands the overwhelming difficulties that many people face as they try to incorporate a healthy lifestyle into one that is already very demanding.

Through her desire to help her young, overweight son, Cheryl embarked on a lengthy personal journey of researching and experimenting to find a healthy weight loss plan. Low fat, low carbohydrate and in particular, calorie counting were among her first attempts to control his weight. Frustration followed as his weight continued to climb to unhealthy levels. Her search ended when she began studying the effects of weight management through low-glycemic eating. She discovered that his calorie consumption was not out of line, but an abundance of high glycemic carbohydrate choices was sabotaging their efforts. With this new found knowledge, Cheryl's next challenge was to adapt and incorporate dietary changes that could fit easily into their busy lifestyle. Her success in this is what motivated her to develop the "Pre-cook Days" and the "Quick Prep" meal plan that can easily be incorporated into any busy household. More importantly, Cheryl encouraged her children to participate in meal preparation. Using an "assembly-line" process, healthy pre-cooked proteins, and an array of low-glycemic carbs, including fresh fruits and vegetables, were lined up on the counter top. Good fats replaced the bad, and homemade snacks replaced rice cakes and instant noodle soups. Her children were taught how to assemble their own personal wraps, pitas and salads for healthy meals on the run. Their involvement allowed them to take ownership of their school lunches while keeping within some healthy boundaries. At the end of each day, Cheryl and her husband were able to put together a quick and delicious meal in minutes.

Another important factor in her son's transformation was the introduction of exercise, replacing some of the hours he normally spent playing video games. As his weight began to reduce, it was evident that the dietary changes and the Quick Prep method were working. It was with some amusement that Cheryl discovered the boys making extra wraps and selling them at school. Parents began to call and ask how the Quick Prep worked. She then realized the need for families and individuals to understand how low-glycemic eating can lead to lifelong weight management and better health. Perhaps even more importantly, her children now have the life skills to prepare healthy meals and include regular exercise as they live on their own as young adults. Whether you are a single person or have a large family to feed, you now have the opportunity to learn how to incorporate homemade healthy "fast food" into your daily meals.

Food preparation, including the availability of healthy food for everyone, has been a part of **Laura Kalina**'s life since early childhood when she had aspirations of becoming a dietitian. Since achieving that dream, her contributions to food security and healthy eating have been many. One of her proudest moments was the opening of Community Kitchens in her city, where families could come together to cook once or twice a week resulting in healthy meals available for their families for all week.

Now a registered dietitian and successful business leader, Laura has an extensive understanding of the role of food and nutrition in the prevention of chronic diseases, such as diabetes, heart disease and cancer. She has seen all too often the damaging effects of oxidative stress on the body caused by hectic lifestyles, poor food choices, environmental pollution and a compromised food production

Laura's children, Anya and Jake, enjoy getting involved in the kitchen – using the Quick Prep method, they can assemble a nutritious school lunch or snack in minutes.

system. As a busy mother herself, with two active teenagers, one of whom is a daughter with type 1 diabetes, she also understands the daunting challenges that families face trying to balance a multitude of activities with the goal of achieving optimal health.

The most common concern of today's busy families is "not enough time." Lack of time, combined with the convenience and prevalence of fast food restaurants and prepackaged foods, has led to an unprecedented rise in obesity rates and chronic diseases such as type 2 diabetes and heart disease. Of particular concern is the tripling of childhood obesity in the last decade. This book will make your "not enough time" concern a thing of the past. It focuses on the "Quick Prep" method and shows you how easy it is to prepare healthy, well-balanced meals for your family in less time than a trip to your local fast food restaurant.

Whatever your nutrition challenge, *Low-Glycemic Meals in Minutes* can start you on the path to a healthier life. It is not just another cookbook; loaded with nutrition tips, cooking suggestions, menu plans and fitness ideas, it will make the transition to well-being easy and fun for you and your family.

Success Stories

JO ANN'S STORY

Nine months ago I was very overweight and struggling with how to deal with it. To make things worse, my doctor gave me the option of taking medication to control my rising blood pressure. At 51 years of age, I wondered how I had got myself to this point. I have always been active — exercising, golfing, curling, walking — how could I be so overweight and now have severe health issues? Whatever the reason, I needed to find a solution.

 The first step of my journey began when I met Cheryl Christian, co-author of this book and a personal trainer. Cheryl helped me develop a fitness and nutrition plan that would fit into my lifestyle. I strength train three days a week with Cheryl and work cardio into my schedule a minimum three days a week at home. Next, I started my nutritional changes with a 5-day low-glycemic fiber cleanse. That led to a nutritional program very similar to Dr. Strand's *Healthy For Life*. I have been following Phase 1 for a consistent weight loss of approximately two pounds per week and have included good quality vitamin and mineral supplements to ensure optimal health.

It has not been easy each and every day, however, I can quite honestly say today, at 51 years of age, I am in better shape than I have been in years. I feel great! What I have learned about health, exercise and nutrition during these past months has definitely changed the way I look at eating and even more importantly, the way I look at exercise. I understand the need to take care of my body today so I will continue to be healthy as I get older. The key is exercise — like it or not. Daily exercise helps slow the aging process and makes us feel and look better. The bonus is weight control. I also understand the importance of choosing lower glycemic foods in my diet. Do I wish I had understood this in my 30s instead of my 50s? Absolutely. However, I also know it is never too late to make healthy changes in your life.

Jo Ann has lost over 50 pounds and almost 60 inches! She has gone from a size 16 to a size 6.

KIM'S STORY

I have been battling my weight most of my life, always unhappy with the way I looked, and consequently missing out on things because of it (wouldn't go swimming with the kids, etc.). The many diet and exercise programs I tried didn't bring me a lot of success. Working out 3 to 4 times a week was making me stronger, but I still couldn't lose that extra 20 or 30 pounds. When I reached

my 50s, I knew I needed to get serious. In June 2005, while at the gym, I overheard Cheryl Christian talking to a friend of mine. She was explaining her "Quick Prep method" which was shopping twice a week and going home and prepping the food right away. This ensured that when you opened your fridge, you had numerous low-glycemic healthy choices which took only 5 or 10 minutes to prepare. That really appealed to me, as I am a very disorganized person.

One thing led to another, and Cheryl became part of my life. I signed her up as my personal trainer and began using her Quick Prep method, incorporating low-glycemic foods into my diet. I learned the importance of proper nutrition and how the Glycemic Index (G.I.) worked. The G.I. made so much sense to me. I broke my meals into 5 or 6 smaller portions and found I was never hungry. Quick Prep was very helpful, as I tend to have a busy schedule. I quickly found out that if I neglected my prep days, I would end up grabbing for something that wasn't a healthy choice.

This time the effort to lose the weight worked! The first 5 pounds didn't make much of an impact on me, because I have lost 5 pounds many times, but when I had lost 10 to 15 pounds, I was starting to feel great and needed to buy new clothes. I looked forward to my training sessions and weekly weigh-ins because of the results I was getting. It's not over yet, but to date I have lost close to 30 pounds. There is no question that it requires effort and hard work, but it's an incredible feeling when you see what you accomplish. It feels even better when you have everyone you know telling you how good you look. There is nothing quite like it!

TOM'S STORY

I am 47 years old and a captain in my city's fire department. Due to a biking accident, I was off work for 6 months, and the inactivity drove my weight up to around 240 pounds. Despite various attempts, I had a hard time losing the extra weight. Then I was introduced by my sister-in-law, a dietitian, to a five-day low-glycemic high-fiber cleanse, which included meal replacement shakes, nutritional bars and quality nutritional supplements. Following the cleanse, I started on a 12-week trim down challenge (similar to the Phase 1 outlined in this book). This lifestyle change has been awesome for me. I wake up in the morning feeling energetic and continue to feel good throughout the day without insatiable carbohydrate cravings. I have the energy to exercise, spend time with my family, and socialize. I feel a renewed youthful exuberance and zest for life.

Tom lost 28 pounds in 12 weeks and now maintains a healthy weight.

Healthy Eating 101

All the recipes in this cookbook were developed to be low to moderate on the glycemic index (G.I.) with emphasis on healthy fats and proteins. The G.I. is simply a numerical system that rates how fast carbohydrates break down into glucose and enter the bloodstream. Low-G.I. foods are slowly digested and absorbed, which causes gentle rises in blood sugar and insulin levels. Lowering your insulin levels is not only a key factor in weight loss, but also the secret to long-term health. Low-G.I. foods, such as fruit, vegetables, legumes (beans and lentils) are also high in fibre, nutrients and antioxidants. Choosing low G.I. foods will help you to:

- control your appetite and cravings, as they tend to keep you feeling fuller, longer
- lose weight
- control your blood glucose levels and lower your risk of getting type 2 diabetes
- control your cholesterol levels and lower your risk of getting heart disease

STOP CARBOHYDRATE CRAVINGS

Carbohydrate cravings often lead to eating high-glycemic foods such as bread, rice, potatoes, commercial baked products and sweets (see table next page). As shown in the graph below, sugar from these foods is digested quickly and causes a rapid spike in blood sugar. This, in turn, triggers a surge of insulin which causes the blood sugar to drop into the hypoglycemic range. This leads to the release of stress hormones, which drives the blood sugar back up to normal but leaves an uncontrollable hunger, resulting in the need to to eat something. Usually it is another high-glycemic meal or snack, continuing the vicious cycle. If you start the day off with a high-glycemic meal, you may eat up to 80% more calories in the day. It is important to observe whether you are spiking your blood sugar with your food choices. Switching to low-glycemic eating will diminish carbohydrate cravings and help control your appetite which will ultimately help you lose weight.

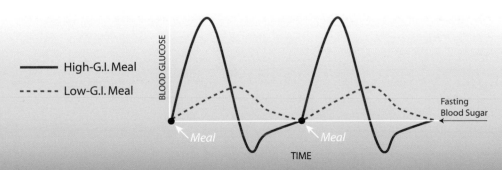

Glycemic Index Tables

The Glycemic Index (G.I.) is a scale that ranks carbohydrate-rich foods by how much they raise blood glucose levels compared to a standard food. The standard food is glucose or white bread. A lot of starchy foods have a high glycemic index.

Choose low- and medium-G.I. foods more often.

Lower G.I. *Choose MOST*	Medium G.I. *Choose MORE often*	Higher G.I. *Choose LEAST*
BREADS		
Sprouted wheat bread or tortilla	Whole grain bread (coarse)	White bread and buns
Oat bran bread	Whole grain rye bread	Whole wheat flour bread
Heavy mixed grain bread	Whole wheat pita	Bagels
Pumpernickel	Whole wheat or flax tortillas	Croissants and baguettes
		Pancakes and waffles
CEREAL		
All Bran™	Grapenuts™	Bran flakes/corn flakes
Bran Buds with Psyllium™	Shredded Wheat™	Rice Krispies™
Slow cook oats	Quick oats	Cheerios™
Oat Bran™		Instant oats
Red River™		Granola
GRAINS		
Barley	Basmati rice	Short-grain and instant rice
Bulgur	Brown rice	Grits
Quinoa	Couscous	Canned pasta
	Parboiled or converted rice	Macaroni and cheese
	Pasta and noodles al dente	Instant noodles
OTHER		
Usana Nutrimeal™	Potato (red or new)	Potato, baking (Russet)
Usana Nutrition Bars™	Sweet corn	French fries
Vegetables	Ryvita™ (rye crisps)	Pretzels
Fruit	Stoned Wheat Thins™	Rice cakes
Black beans	Black bean soup	Soda crackers
Lentils	Green pea soup	Granola bars
Chickpeas	Popcorn	Cake
Kidney beans		Cookies
Split peas		Fruit roll-ups
Soy beans		Candy and pop
Skim milk		Fruit juice
Soy milk		
Yogurt		

For more information on the glycemic index of other foods, go to www.glycemicindex.com

About the Book's Recipes

Low-Glycemic Meals in Minutes is divided into two sections: Quick Prep and 30 Minute Solutions. All of the kitchen tested recipes use the best carbohydrate, protein and fat choices to control hunger, aid in weight loss, maintain blood sugar levels, and improve overall health.

Quick Prep recipes are family friendly and easy to prepare. With the emphasis on precooked proteins, chopped vegetables and a stocked pantry, healthy meals and snacks can be assembled with minimal effort. This book encourages children to feel comfortable in the kitchen and at the same time, teaches them to make healthy food choices.

Recipes from the 30-Minute Solutions section require a little more time to prepare but still remain quick, convenient and uncomplicated.

PHASE 1 AND PHASE 2 GUIDELINES

Individuals following Dr. Strand's *Healthy for Life* or *Releasing Fat* program will find over 125 recipes designed to meet the Phase 1 and Phase 2 guidelines. A sample menu plan is on pages 106 and 107.

Phase 1 eliminates all breads and most grains, cereals, pasta, potatoes and rice. This will help you to reverse your carbohydrate addiction and glycemic stress.

Phase 2 begins to re-introduce the lower-G.I. grains, breads, cereals, pasta and potatoes (red or new) that will not spike blood sugar levels. You will continue to reverse your insulin resistance over time in the majority of cases.

To help you achieve a healthy weight, *Low-Glycemic Meals in Minutes* also features nutrition tips throughout the book and a section on physical activity and cellular nutrition.

With both Cheryl's and Laura's expertise in these areas, you will learn practical suggestions and ideas to incorporate all of these elements into your life. The *Low-Glycemic Meals in Minutes* cookbook will be a valuable tool in your family's journey to optimal health.

Quick Prep

You arrive home after a busy day, ravenous, and without any plans for dinner. The family would love a nutritious home cooked meal, but no one has the time or energy. Have you ever wondered how restaurants can magically prepare many meals in a short time? Wouldn't it be great if you and your family could do the same?

Enter Quick Prep — the healthy meal solution. If you are willing to set aside a couple of hours per week for preparation, this book will show you how to stock your fridge and pantry with quick, ready to assemble meals for your family. This easy system will enable you to have healthy, nutritious meals everyday, in the same amount of time you would spend waiting for a restaurant order.

Better yet, get your family involved in cooking. Invite kids to read the recipes and help collect the necessary ingredients and utensils. Kids can help add ingredients, stir soups and set the table for the meal. Ask them to tell you what they think of the recipe — do they like the taste, color, texture and so on? With the Quick Prep method, kids will feel comfortable in the kitchen and learn how easy it is to assemble a healthy meal in minutes. Who could have imagined that placing your family on the road to well-being could be so easy?

THE QUICK PREP SOLUTION

Step 1 Plan two cook days per week, such as Sunday and Wednesday evenings.

Step 2 Cook two to four protein sources that you will use in Quick Prep recipes over the next three or four days. Amounts prepared will depend on family size. Store in airtight containers and place in fridge for quick meals. If you prefer using dried legumes over canned, prepare a batch and store in airtight containers.

Step 3 • Chop or slice fresh, cleaned vegetables. Place in airtight containers.
  • Prepare a large fresh salad. Try spinach and a variety of mixed greens. (Greens remain fresh and crisp if you add vegetables such as cucumbers, tomatoes, and zucchini just before serving). Store in airtight containers.

Step 4 Prepare salsas, spreads and healthy dressings for the up-coming week using fresh herbs.

You are now ready to assemble healthy meals for the week.

 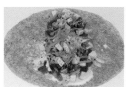  

PREPARING PROTEINS

This section features common protein sources, such as, skinless chicken breasts, ground beef and poultry, canned fish and canned legumes. Broaden your family's menu planning with other healthy proteins such as, lean cuts of beef, lean pork (fat removed), wild game, quail, pheasant, wild salmon, and trout. Vegetarians know the value in other protein sources such as tofu, quinoa, legumes and grains. Look at the easy preparation methods laid out below and decide what proteins you wish to cook.

Poached Chicken Breasts

Skinless, frozen chicken breasts, as opposed to fresh, are often more economical for families. By poaching the chicken breasts, they remain juicy and tender for four days in the fridge.

1. Place skinless, boneless chicken breasts in pot. Cover with water and bring to a boil. Reduce heat and simmer until cooked (approximately 30-40 minutes).

2. Rinse in sink until water runs clear.

3. Place cooked chicken breasts in storage containers and keep up to 4 days in the fridge.

Extra Lean Ground Beef

Ground turkey or chicken can be substituted in many recipes. Experiment!

1. Fry lean ground beef, chicken, turkey until fully cooked (approximately 20 minutes or until no longer pink).

2. Drain off excess fat. You may wish to rinse with hot water if beef has excess fat (optional).

3. Place cooked ground meat or poultry in storage containers for up to 4 days.

Dried Beans, Peas and Lentils (Legumes)

Canned legumes are used in the Quick Prep section. Have a variety on hand in the pantry. You may wish to use dried legumes, as they are very economical, but prepare them on your cooking days to be ready for the coming week.

Dried legumes can be used in place of canned. Follow package directions or instructions on page 93.

13

Fish

Fish is one of your best protein choices, particularly salmon, tuna, trout, mackerel and herring. These fish also provide an excellent source of omega-3 essential fatty acids. Fresh fish is wonderful but not always available, so canned fish is a great staple for your pantry. Cook fresh fish and keep remainder in storage containers for up to 4 days, or have canned fish available for Quick Prep meals.

PREPARING VEGETABLES

Keep an assortment of fresh vegetables, some prepped and ready to use in the Quick Prep recipes.

1. Wash an assortment of fresh vegetables.

2. Cut vegetables such as peppers, onions, and celery for quick use. You may choose to julienne, dice, or chop depending on the recipes you are planning to make.

3. Store in airtight containers.

Salsas and Spreads

Spice up wraps, soups and omelettes with homemade salsas, dressings, fresh herbs and spices.

Prepare salsas and spreads in advance. See pages 37 to 39.

Fresh herbs add flavour without the need to add extra salt, fats or sugars to recipes.

NOTHING GOES TO WASTE

Before you begin the next prep day, use up remaining prepared foods in Clean Sweep soup, salad or stir-fry recipes. Be creative; create your own Clean Sweep recipe.

See recipes on pages 35 and 36.

FRIDGE & FREEZER PREP

Your fridge is now stocked with ready to use vegetables, low-fat proteins and condiments. Complete your fridge prep by having an assortment of fruit, low-fat dairy products, eggs, healthy oils (flaxseed oil), commercial condiments (low-fat mayonnaise, mustards, and low-fat dressings). A well organized fridge helps everyone find the necessary ingredients to make quick and tasty meals.

Your freezer should contain bags of frozen fruit and vegetables, good quality protein sources and ice for smoothies. Purchasing food storage containers in a variety of sizes is a must!

PANTRY

Your pantry should only be stocked with items that are low-glycemic, such as dried or canned legumes, slow cook oats, canned fish, salsas, tomato sauce and condiments. A shopping list has been provided on pages 114 and 115 for photocopying. It has been divided into two sections. You will find the fresh foods list has vegetables, fruit, soy and dairy products and proteins that you will need to restock on a weekly or bi-weekly basis. The pantry list focuses on staples, spices, and condiments for the fridge that will need replenishing less frequently. Avoid shopping without a list or when you are hungry. This will help you avoid the temptation to buy unhealthy snacks.

FOOD SAFETY

To keep food safe to eat and as tasty as possible, it must be stored and reheated properly. Refrigerate leftovers within two hours of preparation. Very hot items should be cooled at room temperature for about 30 minutes before being refrigerated.

Storage Times for Prepared Foods

PRODUCT	REFRIGERATOR (40°F/4°C)	FREEZER (0°F/-17°C)
Cooked chicken pieces, plain	up to 4 days	up to 1 month
Cooked ground meat, meatloaf and meat casseroles	up to 4 days	up to 3 months
Soups and stews	up to 3 days	up to 6 months
Cooked poultry casseroles	up to 4 days	up to 4 months
Cooked fish	up to 4 days	up to 6 months
Combination dishes (such as lasagna)	up to 4 days	up to 6 months

Mocha Latte Smoothie

Quick Prep

Quick Prep Nutrition Shakes

Avoid the "I don't have time for breakfast" routine! Breakfast is truly one of the most important meals of the day. If you eat a low-glycemic breakfast you will have fewer carbohydrate cravings all day. With diminished carbohydrate cravings you can control your appetite, which will ultimately help you achieve a healthy weight. The following recipes take only minutes to make — so start your day off right!

Phase 1 Shakes

LOW-GLYCEMIC SHAKE
Makes 1 serving

2 cups water
½ cup frozen berries
2 oz (60 g) strawberry or vanilla
   meal replacement powder
2 cups ice
1 tbsp ground flaxseed

In a blender, combine all ingredients and blend until smooth.

STRAWBERRY BANANA SMOOTHIE
Makes 1 serving

1 cup low-fat milk
½ cup strawberries
½ banana
1 oz (30 g) soy protein or pure whey powder
2 cups ice

In a blender, combine all ingredients and blend until smooth.

ORANGE CREAMSICLE SHAKE
Makes 1 serving

¼ cup orange juice
½ banana
2 oz (60 g) vanilla flavoured
   meal replacement powder
1½ cups water
2 cups ice

In a blender, combine all ingredients and blend until smooth.

MOCHA LATTE SMOOTHIE
Makes 1 serving

1 cup cold coffee
1 cup low fat milk
2 oz (60 g) chocolate flavoured
   meal replacement powder
2 cups ice

In a blender, combine all ingredients and blend until smooth.

Nutrition Tip

Look for low-glycemic meal replacements which provide approximately 15 grams of protein per serving. One 60 gram serving equals 3 scoops, or 1 meal replacement package.

Phase 1 Shakes

SHAKE ON THE RUN

Makes 1 serving

1 cup water or milk
1 container (175 g) sugar-free fruit yogurt
2 oz (60 g) vanilla or strawberry
    meal replacement powder
1 to 2 cups ice

Add all ingredients to blender bottle and shake.

CHOCOLATE BANANA MALT

Makes 1 serving

1 cup low fat milk
½ banana
2 oz (60 g) chocolate flavoured meal
    replacement powder
1 tsp cocoa powder
2 cups ice

In a blender, combine all ingredients and blend until smooth.

PUMPKIN PIE SHAKE

Makes 1 serving

½ cup water
1 cup skim milk
2 oz (60 g) vanilla or cappuccino flavoured
    meal replacement powder
4 tbsp pumpkin purée
¼ tsp each of cinnamon, allspice and nutmeg
1 to 2 cups ice

In blender, combine all ingredients and blend until smooth.

JAKE'S SHAKE

Makes 1 serving

½ cup low-fat milk
1 cup water
2 oz (60g) vanilla flavoured meal replacement
    powder
½ banana
½ cup unsweetened frozen mixed fruit
    (optional)
1 single-serve low-calorie drink mix such as
    Nestea® (optional)
2 cups ice

In a blender combine all ingredients and blend until smooth.

PEANUT BUTTER CUP SMOOTHIE

Makes 1 serving

1 cup water
1 cup low-fat milk
2 oz (60g) chocolate flavoured
    meal replacement powder
2 tbsp natural peanut butter
2 cups ice

In a blender, combine all ingredients and blend until smooth.

Nutrition Tip

For a quick and satisfying snack, try one tablespoon of peanut butter on a celery stick or sprouted wheat bread. Peanuts provide a plant source of protein, healthy monounsaturated fat, vitamins, and fiber. Almond butter and cashew butter are also tasty choices. Look for those products that are natural and non-hydrogenated.

Phase 2 Shakes

SUNRISE HIGH ENERGY SMOOTHIE

Makes 1 serving

½ cup water
½ cup low-fat vanilla yogurt
½ cup fresh or unsweetened frozen fruit
   (strawberries, blueberries, raspberries,
   blackberries)
¼ cup orange juice
2 oz (60 g) strawberry or vanilla
   meal replacement powder
1 tbsp ground flaxseed or flaxseed oil
2 cups ice

In a blender, combine all ingredients and blend until smooth.

TROPICAL CHEESECAKE SMOOTHIE

Makes 2 servings

1 can (10 oz/284 ml) mandarin orange
   segments with juice
1 can (14 oz/398 ml) pineapple in its own juice
1 cup low-fat cottage cheese or plain yogurt
½ cup orange juice
2 cups ice

In a blender, combine all ingredients and blend until smooth.

BANANARAMA TOFU BOOST

Makes 1 serving

1 ripe banana
½ cup dessert tofu (or fruit flavoured)
2 oz (60 g) vanilla flavoured meal replacement
   powder
1 cup low-fat milk
¼ tsp almond extract
1 cup ice

In a blender, combine all ingredients and blend until smooth.

LEMON TART SMOOTHIE

Makes 1 serving

½ cup low-fat plain yogurt
1 tbsp lemon juice
½ cup unsweetened frozen strawberries,
   thawed
1 cup unsweetened grape juice or light
   cranberry/raspberry juice
1 oz (30 g) soya protein powder
2 cups ice

In a blender, combine all ingredients and blend until smooth.

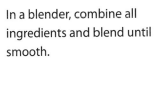

Strawberry Banana Smoothie

Quick Breakfast Ideas

ON-THE-RUN BREAKFAST

Phase 2 • Makes 1 serving

½ cup All-Bran™ or Bran Buds™
1 cup fresh fruit
½ cup cottage cheese (1% or fat-free)
2 tbsp sliced almonds

Mix in a bowl and enjoy.

EGG IN A NEST (KID FRIENDLY)

Phase 2 • Makes 1 serving

1 slice whole grain bread
1 egg
2 tbsp cheddar cheese, grated
salt and pepper to taste

Coat frying pan with non-stick spray and heat over medium heat. Cut out center of bread in the shape of a circle (using a glass or a cookie cutter). Place bread into frying pan and break egg into center. Cover with lid, reduce heat to low, and cook until egg is done. Sprinkle cheese on top. Serve with salsa if desired.

COUNTRY GARDEN OMELETTE

Phase 1 • Makes 2 servings

✦ *Sauté in a 10-inch non-stick frying pan and cook until softened:*
   1 tbsp olive oil
   ½ cup assorted vegetables, finely chopped
      (onion, green or red bell pepper)

✦ *Beat together:*
   3 eggs
   2 tbsp skim milk
   dash dried oregano and basil
   salt and pepper to taste
   2 tbsp sharp cheddar cheese, grated

Pour egg mixture over vegetables in pan and reduce heat to low. Cover and cook for a few minutes until eggs are fluffy and no longer runny. Top with grated cheese and cover for 1 minute.

For Phase 2, make a wrap by cutting omelette in pieces and placing in two 10-inch whole wheat or flaxseed tortillas. Top with salsa. Roll up and enjoy.

Country Garden Omelette

OLD FASHIONED OATMEAL

Phase 1 • Makes 2 servings

1 cup slow cook oats
1¾ cup water or skim milk
½ cup dried cranberries
2 tbsp sliced almonds, toasted

Bring water to boil, add oats and cranberries. Cover, turn off heat and let sit for 10 to 12 minutes without stirring. Add almonds just before serving.

HOMEMADE MUESLI

Phase 1 • Makes 2 servings

1 cup slow cook oats
¾ cup skim milk
¾ cup low-fat, sugar-free fruit yogurt
2 tbsp sliced almonds
¾ cup diced apple, pear or berries
sweetener to taste

In bowl, soak oats in milk. Place in refrigerator overnight. Add yogurt, almonds, fruit and sweetener to taste. Mix well.

FRENCH TOAST

Phase 2 • Makes 2 servings

1 egg
2 tbsp low-fat milk
½ tsp cinnamon
½ tsp pure vanilla extract
2 slices sprouted wheat bread

In a shallow dish, whisk egg, milk, cinnamon and vanilla. Dip 2 slices of bread into egg mixture. Cook in a non-stick frying pan on medium to high heat until lightly browned.

May serve with peanut butter and light jam, or yogurt and fruit.

Nutrition Tip

Eggs are high in protein and contain valuable nutrients such as vitamin A, magnesium, iron and riboflavin. Look for omega-3 enriched eggs. While more expensive than regular eggs, they are lower in saturated fat, higher in omega-3 fatty acids and contain more Vitamin E.

Spicy Pineapple Chicken

Quick Prep Meals

Quick Prep Poultry

These recipes use skinless, pre-cooked poultry that has been poached. Refer to cooking instructions on page 13. Many recipes are "kid friendly"— especially great for teens who arrive home hungry after school. These recipes are also great for entertaining unexpected company— a delicious meal ready in minutes.

Refer to cooking instructions on page 13.

Poultry

SPICY PINEAPPLE CHICKEN

Phase 1 • Makes 4 servings

✦ **Sauté 5 to 7 minutes in a large frying pan:**
  1 tbsp olive oil
  1 red bell pepper, cut in strips,
  1 green bell pepper, cut in strips,

✦ **Add:**
  1 can (14 oz/398 ml) pineapple chunks with juice
  1 cup salsa
  2 tbsp cilantro or parsley, chopped
  2 tsp grated fresh ginger or ¾ tsp ground ginger
  2 cups cooked chicken, cubed

Continue to cook stirring frequently, until chicken is heated through. For a thicker sauce, mix 1 tsp cornstarch with 3 tbsp water and add to pan. Heat until thickened, stirring constantly. Add salt and pepper to taste.

Try serving over lightly cooked bean sprouts or chopped chinese greens for additional flavour.

QUICK CHICKEN SOUP

Phase 2 • Makes 4 to 6 servings

✦ **Sauté in large pot until tender:**
  1 tbsp olive oil
  1 onion, chopped
  2 stalks celery, chopped
  2 carrots, chopped

  Sprinkle 2 tbsp all-purpose flour over vegetables and stir for 2 minutes.

✦ **Add and bring to a boil:**
  4 cups or 1 carton (32 oz/900 ml) chicken broth
  3 cups low-fat milk
  ¼ tsp each of dried sage, thyme and savory
  1 tsp Worcestershire sauce
  2 cups cooked chicken breast, diced

✦ **Add:**
  ½ cup uncooked whole wheat pasta.

  Reduce heat and simmer for 15 to 20 minutes.

Tips to Improve Your Kids' Nutrition

• Make a conscious effort to eat together as a family and keep meal times pleasant.
• Remember, parents are role models for healthy lifestyles.
• Monitor screen time (computer/TV). Not only are kids inactive in front of a screen, they are influenced by commercials for junk food. They will snack more while sitting in front of a screen than when they are playing.
• Have a general rule not to eat food anywhere in the house except in the kitchen or dining room.

THAI CHICKEN TORTILLA PIZZA
Phase 2 • Makes 4 to 6 servings

Preheat oven to 375°F.

✦ *Bake for 3 minutes on an ungreased cookie sheet:*
4 whole wheat tortillas

✦ *Spread on each tortilla:*
1 to 2 tbsp Thai Peanut Sauce (page 38) or your favourite store-bought light peanut sauce

✦ *Sprinkle evenly over all 4 tortillas:*
2 cups cooked chicken, finely chopped
½ small red bell pepper, julienned
½ small green bell pepper, julienned
½ cup carrots, grated
1 cup low-fat mozzarella cheese, grated

Bake 10 to 12 minutes until cheese is completely melted and edges are lightly browned. If desired, broil for one minute to brown top. Use a pizza cutter to cut into wedges.

ASIAN SALAD
Phase 1 • Makes 4 servings

✦ *Toss together in a large bowl:*
2 cups cooked chicken, cubed
3 cups shredded cabbage
1 cup mushrooms, sliced
2 carrots, grated
2 tbsp cilantro, chopped
1 cucumber, thinly sliced
½ cup non-fat oriental style salad dressing or Ginger-Sesame Dressing on page 56
black pepper to taste

✦ *Top with:*
3 green onions, thinly sliced
1 tangerine, divided into sections

DIJON CHICKEN
Phase 1 served over salad greens
Phase 2 served over rice or whole wheat pasta
Makes 4 servings

✦ *Sauté in a large frying pan, over medium heat:*
1 tomato, seeded and chopped
2 green onions, chopped
1 green bell pepper, sliced
¼ cup cilantro, chopped
⅓ cup dijon mustard
2 tbsp fresh lime juice
2 cups cooked chicken breasts, cubed

You can substitute 1 cup of Big Batch Tomato Salsa (page 37) for the tomato, onion, pepper and cilantro.

Thai Chicken Tortilla Pizza

INDONESIAN CURRIED SALAD

Phase 1 · Makes 4 servings

✦ *Stir together in a medium size bowl:*
2 cups cooked chicken, cubed
2 pears with skin, cubed
½ English cucumber with skin, chopped
2 green onions, chopped

CURRY DRESSING

✦ *Whisk together:*
¼ cup low-fat plain yogurt
¼ cup low-fat mayonnaise
1 tsp curry powder
½ tsp dry mustard
½ tsp ground allspice
½ tsp garlic powder
salt and pepper to taste

Stir chicken mixture and dressing together.
Serve over salad greens.

TURKEY PESTO QUESADILLAS

Phase 2 · Makes 4 to 6 servings

Preheat oven to 350°F.

✦ *Arrange in a single layer on baking sheet:*
4 large whole wheat tortillas

✦ *Top half a side of each tortilla evenly with:*
1 tbsp pesto (store-bought)
¼ cup parmesan cheese, grated
½ cup onion, chopped
1 large tomato, seeded and sliced
½ cup black olives, sliced
2 cups cooked turkey or chicken, chopped
1 pkg (10 oz/300 g) frozen chopped spinach,
   thawed with moisture squeezed out
½ cup feta cheese, crumbled
¾ cup low-fat mozzarella cheese, grated

Fold each tortilla over. Bake 15 to 20 minutes,
or until tortillas are golden and cheese is
melted. Cut each quesadilla into 6 wedges
and serve with salsa and low-fat sour cream,
if desired.

*Quesadillas are good for lunches or snacks, and
make a great party platter when cut into small
wedges and arranged with small bowls of salsa
and sour cream.*

Indonesian Curried Salad

Turkey Cacciatore with Peppers

Phase 1 • Makes 4 servings

✦ *Sauté in a large non-stick frying pan for about 5 minutes until softened:*

1 tbsp olive oil

4 cloves garlic, minced

2 stalks celery, diced

1 large onion, chopped

1 red bell pepper, julienned

1 green bell pepper, julienned

½ tsp dried oregano

½ tsp dried thyme

✦ *Add:*

1 can (19 oz/540 ml) diced tomatoes

✦ *Whisk together:*

2 tbsp flour

1½ cup skim or 1% milk

Add to ingredients in frying pan, stirring constantly and heat until thickened (2 to 3 minutes).

✦ *Add:*

2 cups of cooked turkey, cubed

½ tsp each salt and pepper

Heat thoroughly. Serve with grated parmesan cheese.

Fast Fusion Chicken

Phase 1 • Makes 4 to 6 servings

✦ *Saute in a large, non-stick frying pan at medium-high heat until browned:*

1 to 2 tbsp olive oil

2 cups cooked chicken breast, cubed

½ large onion, chopped

2 cloves garlic, minced

✦ *Add and toss until thoroughly coated:*

1 tbsp curry powder

✦ *Add:*

1 red bell pepper, chopped

1¼ cups low-sodium chicken broth

⅓ cup raisins

2 tbsp tomato paste

1 tbsp lime juice

Reduce heat and simmer for 15 to 20 minutes or until thickened. Serve with side salad.

Phase 2 if served over basmati rice.

Nutrition Tip

Recipes like Turkey Cacciatore with Peppers provide two sources of protein: turkey and milk. Protein is an essential nutrient because it helps build and repair muscle, hair, nails and skin. Protein also lowers the glycemic index of a meal, which helps control blood sugar.

Quick Prep Ground Meats

Having cooked ground beef on hand makes it easy to come up with a quick meal solution. The recipes use extra lean ground beef that has been cooked and drained. You may substitute ground poultry or ground wild game. Always ensure that you have thoroughly cooked your ground beef, and then refrigerate.

MEDITERRANEAN PITA PIZZA

Phase 2 • Makes 4 to 6 servings

Preheat oven to 375°F.

✦ **Bake on a cookie sheet for 5 minutes until crisp:**
4 large whole wheat pitas

✦ **Mix:**
2 cups cooked ground beef, well crumbled
1 medium onion, minced
½ cup tomato sauce
1 tsp dried oregano
1 tsp dried basil
½ tsp each salt and pepper

✦ **Combine in separate bowl:**
1 large tomato, chopped
½ cup feta cheese (or mozzarella), crumbled
½ cup parmesan cheese, grated

✦ **Prepare garnish of:**
⅓ cup black olives, sliced

Layer a quarter of the meat filling onto each pita, then do the same with the tomato/cheese mixture. Sprinkle tops with sliced olives. Bake 12 to 15 minutes.

GROUND BEEF STROGANOFF

Phase 1 • Makes 4 servings

✦ **Sauté in a non-stick pan:**
1 tbsp olive oil
1 onion, chopped
2 cloves garlic, chopped
1 green or red bell pepper, diced
2 cups fresh or 1 can (10 oz/284 ml) mushrooms, reserve juice

✦ **Add and simmer until heated through:**
2 cups ground beef, cooked
1 tbsp paprika
1 cup liquid (juice from canned mushrooms plus beef broth to make 1 cup)

✦ **Mix together:**
1 tbsp flour
4 tbsp low-fat sour cream or plain yogurt

Stir into stroganoff. Heat until sauce thickens.

Phase 2 if served with low-glycemic rice such as basmati, parboiled or brown, or over whole wheat pasta.

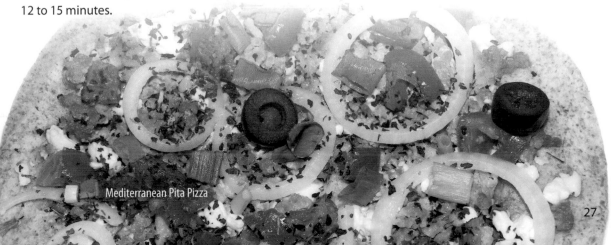
Mediterranean Pita Pizza

Jiffy Ground Beef Stir-Fry

Phase 1 • Makes 4 servings

✦ **Sauté in a large non-stick frying pan over medium heat:**
1 tbsp olive oil
1 onion, chopped
3 cloves garlic, chopped
1 red bell pepper, julienned
2 cups broccoli, tops broken into florets and stems sliced

✦ **Add, then heat throughout:**
2 cups ground beef, cooked
1 tbsp fresh ginger, grated (or 1 tsp powdered ginger)
1 tbsp wine vinegar
¼ cup soy sauce
1 can (14 oz/398 ml) pineapple chunks, with juice

✦ **Blend in a small bowl:**
2 tsp cornstarch
¼ cup water

Add to beef mixture and stir until heated through.

Phase 2 if served over low-glycemic rice, such as basmati, parboiled or brown.

Quick Chili

Phase 1 • Makes 6 servings

✦ **Sauté in a stock pot:**
1 tbsp olive oil
1 onion, chopped
1 green bell pepper, chopped
3 cloves garlic, minced

✦ **Add:**
2 cups ground beef or chicken, cooked
1 can (19 oz/540 ml) kidney beans, drained and rinsed
1 can (19 oz/540 ml) romano beans, drained and rinsed
1 can (28 oz/796 ml) diced tomatoes with juice
1 can (5½ oz/156 ml) tomato paste
2 cups water
1 can (10 oz/284 ml) sliced mushrooms, drained
1 to 2 tbsp chili powder (as desired)
1 tsp ground cumin
½ tsp salt

Bring to a boil, then simmer 20 minutes uncovered, stirring often.

Quick Chilli

LETTUCE WRAPS

Phase 1 • Makes 4 servings

Wash one head of iceberg lettuce, dry and separate the leaves. Set aside.

✦ *Heat in a medium saucepan:*
  2 cups cooked ground beef
  2 green onions, chopped
  1 red bell pepper, diced
  1 can (7 oz/227 ml) water chestnuts, drained and chopped

✦ *Add:*
  ½ cup Thai Peanut Sauce (page 38) or your favourite store-bought light peanut sauce.
  2 tbsp hoisin sauce
  ½ English cucumber, finely chopped
  1 carrot, grated

Serve mixture in lettuce leaves by spooning a tablespoon into the middle. Lettuce wraps are designed to be eaten "taco-style."

TACO SALAD IN A TORTILLA BOWL

Phase 2 • Makes 4 servings

Preheat oven to 375°F.

Form 4 small whole wheat tortillas into 4 fluted baking pans or 4 oven-proof 6-inch pyrex glass bowls. Bake 8 to 10 minutes or until lightly browned. Set aside.

✦ *Sauté for 5 to 7 minutes:*
  1 tbsp olive oil
  1 small onion, chopped
  1 clove garlic, minced
  2 stalks celery, chopped

✦ *Add and heat throughout:*
  2 cups cooked ground beef
  1 cup salsa (store-bought or recipe page 37)

Layer tortilla bowl with meat mixture, store-bought refried beans or Black Bean Salsa (page 37) and shredded lettuce.

Garnish with low-fat sour cream, grated light cheddar cheese, and additional salsa if desired.

Taco Salad in a Tortilla Bowl

Tomato Spaghetti Sauce

Phase 1 served over spaghetti squash strands
Phase 2 served over cooked whole wheat pasta
    (½ cup per serving)
Makes 4 to 6 servings

✦ **Sauté in a large pot:**

1 tbsp olive oil
1 medium onion, chopped
2 stalks celery, chopped
2 cups fresh mushrooms, chopped
    or 1 can (10 oz/284 ml) drained
2 cloves garlic, minced

✦ **Add:**

1 can (5½ oz/156 ml) tomato paste
1 can (5½ oz/156 ml) water
1 can (28 oz/796 ml) diced tomatoes with juice
2 cups cooked ground meat
1 tsp dried basil leaves
2 tsp dried oregano leaves
1 tsp salt
½ tsp pepper

Simmer for 30 minutes or longer. Sprinkle with parmesan cheese when serving.

Hamburger Soup

Phase 1 • Makes 12 servings, 1 cup each

✦ **In a large stock pot on medium heat, mix:**

2 cups cooked ground beef
1 can (28 oz/798 ml) diced tomatoes
1 can (19 oz/540 ml) kidney beans
1 can (10 oz/284 ml)) tomato sauce
1 can (10 oz/284 ml) mushrooms, drained
5 cups water
1 medium onion, chopped
2 carrots, chopped
2 celery stalks, chopped
1 tsp Worcestershire sauce
½ tsp hot pepper sauce
½ tsp freshly ground pepper

Bring to boil. Reduce heat and simmer covered for about 35 minutes.

✦ **Add:**

2 small zucchini, chopped

Simmer 10 minutes longer. Serve.

For Phase 2 add ½ cup whole wheat pasta or barley. If using barley, add with vegetables. If using pasta, add with zucchini.

Tomato Spaghetti Sauce

Quick Prep Canned or Cooked Fish

Fish

We do not always have the luxury of fresh fish, so the following recipes feature canned fish. Leftover fresh fish can be substituted in any of the recipes, just match quantities of the fresh fish to tin sizes. When tasty food is easy to make, older kids and teens will get into the action. Quick Prep makes the healthy choice the easy choice, and will curtail the endless trips to the cupboard at snack time for chips, cookies and crackers.

TUNA SALAD MIX

Phase 1 with lettuce or salad
Phase 2 in wrap or pita
Makes 3 to 4 servings

✦ *Mix:*

2 tins (6 oz/184 g each) water packed tuna, drained
¼ cup low-fat mayonnaise
2 dill pickles, chopped
2 green onions, minced
1 celery stalk, chopped

Serve over a bed of lettuce greens, in wraps or in pitas.

Teens can make this as a nutritious after school snack. It is easy to make, low-glycemic and low-fat.

CURRIED TUNA PIZZA

Phase 2 • Makes 4 servings

✦ *Mix:*

⅓ cup low-fat mayonnaise
1 tsp lemon juice
½ tsp curry powder

✦ *Add:*

1 tin (6 oz/184 g) water packed tuna, drained
1 stalk celery, finely chopped

✦ *Spread mixture over:*

4 whole wheat tortillas, 6-inch

✦ *Sprinkle evenly with:*

1 cup low-fat mozzarella cheese, grated
2 green onions, chopped

Broil 4 to 5 minutes or until lightly browned.

TUNA BURGER

Phase 1 served with salad
Phase 2 in whole grain bun or pita
Makes 4 servings

✦ *Mix:*

2 tins (6 oz/184 g each) water packed tuna, drained
1 egg
1 cup whole wheat bread crumbs
1 small onion, chopped
2 cloves garlic, minced
1 tbsp soy sauce
1 tbsp light teriyaki sauce
1 tbsp ketchup

Shape into patties. Sprinkle ½ cup cornmeal on a dish and coat patties on each side. Fry patties in 1 tbsp olive oil for about 6 minutes per side or until browned and heated through. Serve with a fresh lemon wedge and Light Tartar Sauce (page 39), or in a whole wheat bun or pita.

Nutrition Tip

The health benefits of fish have been widely established; it is a relatively inexpensive source of high-quality protein, low in saturated fat and contains omega-3 fatty acids, touted for their heart-protective benefits. Predatory fish such as shark, swordfish, fresh and frozen tuna, albacore tuna (not canned light tuna), have higher levels of mercury and should be consumed only occasionally. Canned light tuna contains species of tuna such as skipjack, yellow fin, and tongol, which are relatively low in mercury. Canned light tuna also tends to be lower in price which is an added bonus.

Italian Tuna Sauce

Phase 1 served over spaghetti squash strands
Phase 2 served over cooked whole wheat pasta
Makes 4 servings

✦ **Bring to boil:**
1 can (19 oz/540 ml) stewed tomatoes
1 zucchini, chopped
1 tsp garlic, crushed
1 tsp Italian seasoning

✦ **Add:**
2 tins (6 oz/184 g each) water packed tuna,
  drained

Boil gently, uncovered, stirring often until thickened.

Toss with 2 cups spaghetti squash strands (Phase 1) or 2 cups cooked whole wheat pasta (Phase 2). Sprinkle with fresh or grated parmesan cheese.

Nutrition Tip

Salmon is an excellent source of omega-3 fat. Research has shown that omega-3 fat in fish helps protect us against heart disease and cancer, and that fish oil can enhance the immune system and suppress cancer cell growth. The best way to get omega-3s is by eating cold water fish such as salmon, trout and sardines. To boost your omega-3s, take a pharmaceutical grade fish oil supplement.

Salmon Salad Fajitas

Phase 1 served over shredded lettuce
Phase 2 in whole wheat tortillas or pitas
Makes 4 servings

✦ **Combine in a mixing bowl:**
1 tin (7½ oz/231 g) salmon, drained
2 tbsp low-fat mayonnaise
¼ cup low-fat plain yogurt
¼ tsp chili powder

✦ **Add, stirring gently:**
1 carrot, grated
1 green onion, chopped
1 tomato, diced
½ cucumber, diced
¼ cup cilantro leaves, chopped
salt and pepper to taste

Salmon Waldorf Salad

Phase 1 • Makes 4 servings

✦ **Combine in a bowl:**
2 tins (7½ oz/231 g each) salmon, drained
2 celery stalks, diced
1 large apple, chopped
½ cup walnuts, broken

DRESSING

✦ **Stir together in a separate bowl:**
½ cup low-fat mayonnaise
¼ cup low-fat plain yogurt
1 tsp lemon juice
½ tsp dried thyme
¼ tsp each salt and pepper

Stir dressing into salad and serve.

SALMON LOAF

Phase 2 • Makes 4 to 6 servings

Preheat oven to 350°F.

✦ *Mix:*

2 cups leftover cooked fish or 2 tins
  (7½ oz/231 g each) salmon, drained
½ cup whole wheat bread crumbs
2 eggs, beaten
1 cup milk
1 tsp dill weed
1 cup onion, finely chopped
1 cup celery, finely chopped
5 shakes of Tabasco sauce
1 tsp salt (if not using canned fish)

Place mixture into a loaf pan or muffin tins
sprayed with cooking spray. Bake 40 minutes
for a loaf or 25 minutes in muffin tins.

TUNA CITRUS SPINACH SALAD

Phase 1 • Makes 4 servings

✦ *In a large bowl combine:*

1 can (10 oz/284 ml) mandarin oranges,
  drained
5 cups baby spinach leaves, washed and torn
  into pieces
½ Spanish onion, thinly sliced in rings
2 tins (6 oz/184 g each) solid water packed
  tuna, drained

DRESSING

✦ *Mix in a glass jar:*

1 tbsp sugar
½ tsp salt
1 tbsp dijon mustard
2 tsp lemon rind, grated
¼ cup fresh lemon juice (juice of 1 lemon)
2 tbsp flaxseed oil

Pour dressing over salad, toss to coat. Sprinkle
with ⅓ cup toasted almonds.

Tuna Citrus Spinach Salad

Mix and Match Wraps and Pitas

Mix and Match is a wonderful way to teach children how to prepare healthy lunches and snacks. By adding ingredients in an assembly line fashion, kids can choose their favourite fillings and toppings. Mix and Match recipes are Phase 2. For a Phase 1 recipe, use a lettuce leaf to wrap.

Choose a whole grain, flax, or sprouted wheat tortilla or pita pocket. Preheat in a microwave for 5 to 10 seconds before filling to make it easier to roll.

STEP 1
Place 2 to 3 oz (approximately ⅓ cup) protein of your choice onto the bottom third of each wrap or inside a pita.

STEP 2
Add your favourite chopped vegetables or fruit.

STEP 3
Dress it up with salsas, spreads or sauces (see pages 37 to 39).

STEP 4
Sprinkle with your favorite extras.

STEP 5
Wrap by folding in two sides, then folding bottom up over filling and roll until tight.

STEP 1 PROTEIN	STEP 2 VEGGIES/FRUIT	STEP 3 DRESSING	STEP 4 EXTRAS
Ground beef	Tomato Lettuce	Tzatziki Sauce (page 38) Hummus	Feta cheese
Chicken	Bean sprouts Onion Carrots	Black Bean Salsa (page 37) Tomato Salsa (page 37)	Low-fat cheese
Turkey	Bell peppers	Thai Peanut Sauce (page 38)	Hot sauce
Fish canned or fresh (tuna, salmon)	Avocado	Low-fat sour cream Natural peanut butter Sesame seed butter	Olives
Eggs	Celery	Low-fat mayonnaise	Pickles
Tofu	Zucchini Mushrooms	Low-fat commercial dressings	Spices
Legumes	Pineapple		
Cottage cheese	Strawberries Apples Pears Bananas	Low-fat plain yogurt	

Quick Prep "Clean Sweep" Leftovers

After 3 to 4 days, you are likely to have some odds and ends left in the fridge. There is no need to discard them if the vegetables and proteins have remained fresh. The following recipes are just a few ways to use up the remaining Quick Prep foods in a stir-fry, soup or salad. Experiment and create your own unique recipe!

CLEAN SWEEP STIR-FRY

Phase 1 • Makes 4 to 6 servings

✦ **Whisk in a glass bowl then set aside:**
1 tbsp soy sauce
⅓ cup orange juice
2 tbsp hoisin sauce
½ tsp cornstarch

✦ **Slice:**
5 to 6 cups assorted vegetables (red and green bell peppers, carrots, celery, zucchini, cauliflower, broccoli, mushrooms, bean sprouts, snow peas, peas, green beans, shredded cabbage or water chestnuts)

✦ **Sauté in a large frying pan or wok over medium-high heat:**
1 tbsp olive oil
2 small onions, cut into wedges
1 clove garlic, minced
1 tbsp fresh ginger, chopped

Add firmer vegetables first, stirring constantly. Add remaining softer vegetables and cook 2 to 3 minutes or until firm vegetables are tender crisp. Pour soy mixture into vegetables. Cook 1 to 2 minutes or until thickened. Sprinkle with toasted almonds or sesame seeds.

Option: Add any available protein (chicken, beef) to make a complete meal.

CLEAN SWEEP SOUP

Phase 1 • Makes 5 to 6 servings

✦ **Sauté in a stock pot until soft:**
1 tbsp olive oil
1 medium onion, chopped
3 cloves garlic, chopped

✦ **Add:**
10 cups chicken, beef or vegetable stock
5 cups assorted vegetables, chopped (green bell peppers, diced tomatoes, cabbage, carrots, celery, green beans, etc.)
¼ cup parsley, chopped
1 tsp each salt and pepper
1 tsp dried thyme
1 tsp oregano
1 bay leaf
Worcestershire, hot sauce or salsa to taste

Bring to a boil, reduce heat. Cover and simmer for 45 minutes to 1 hour or until vegetables are tender.

Options:
• *Add left over protein, such as turkey, chicken, beef, or tofu to this soup for a complete meal.*
• *Add 1 can (19 oz/540 ml) beans, dried split peas or lentils to increase protein content.*
• *For a Phase 2 recipe, add ½ cup rice, ½ cup whole wheat pasta or ⅓ cup barley.*

Clean Sweep Salad

Clean Sweep Stir-fry

CLEAN SWEEP SALAD

Phase 1 • Makes 4 to 6 servings

✦ ***Mix in a bowl:***
   3 cups salad greens
   1 red onion, sliced
   3 cups vegetables, chopped (red, green or
      yellow bell peppers, broccoli, cauliflower,
      grated carrot, celery, tomato, cucumber)
   ½ cup feta cheese, crumbled

   DRESSING

✦ ***Mix:***
   ¼ cup fresh lemon juice (juice of 1 lemon)
   2 tbsp olive oil
   1 clove garlic, minced
   2 tbsp dried oregano, crumbled

   Pour dressing over vegetables.

   *Add leftover protein such as chicken, turkey, beef
   or eggs for a complete meal.*

CLEAN SWEEP COLESLAW

✦ ***Toss together in a large bowl:***
   7 to 8 cups green or purple cabbage, shredded
   1 cup carrots, grated

   ORANGE VINAIGRETTE DRESSING

✦ ***Mix in a small bowl:***
   2 cloves garlic, crushed
   1 tbsp dried parsley
   ¼ cup white vinegar
   ½ cup orange juice
   ¼ cup flax oil
   2 tsp sugar or sweetener of choice
   ½ tsp salt
   freshly ground pepper to taste

   NUT TOPPING (OPTIONAL)

✦ ***Combine in a small bowl:***
   ¼ cup sunflower seeds
   ¼ cup pumpkin seeds
   ¼ cup dried soya nuts
   ½ cup sliced almonds

   Pour 2 to 3 tbsp of dressing over 1 to 2 cups of
   coleslaw mixture. Top with 2 tbsp nut topping.

   *Store-bought bags of coleslaw mix make
   this salad extremely quick to prepare. There
   will be enough dressing for additional salads
   throughout the week.*

Clean Sweep Soup

Quick Prep Salsas, Spreads and Dips

A great way to enhance the flavour of many dishes is to keep fresh salsas and spreads at your fingertips. If you take the time to prepare some of the low-G.I. recipes in this section, you will have a variety of mix-and-match sauces for the up-coming week. Spice up wraps, pitas and meals with a burst of flavour!

BIG BATCH TOMATO SALSA

Phase 1

✦ *In a large non-metal bowl combine:*
  6 large tomatoes, seeded and diced
  2 red bell peppers, minced
  2 green bell peppers, minced
  1 sweet white onion, minced
  1 tsp jalapeno pepper, minced
  ½ cup white vinegar
  1 can (5.5 oz/156 ml) tomato paste (use only if you want thicker salsa)
  4 garlic cloves, minced
  ½ cup fresh cilantro, chopped (optional)
  3 tbsp lime juice (fresh squeezed is best)
  2 tbsp lemon juice (fresh squeezed if possible)
  1 tsp chili powder
  1½ tsp dried oregano
  1 tbsp dried parsley
  1 tsp salt
  1 tsp pepper

Cover and refrigerate for at least 1 hour, or overnight for flavours to blend. Keeps up to 4 days refrigerated.

This salsa can be used as a dip, or in pitas, wraps, omelettes, chili and taco bowls, and in "clean sweep" recipes. Be creative!

BLACK BEAN SALSA

Phase 1

✦ *Combine in a medium bowl:*
  1 can (19 oz/540 ml) black beans, rinsed and drained
  1 can (12 oz/341 ml) corn kernels, drained
  2 tomatoes, diced
  1 small onion, finely chopped
  1 tbsp olive oil
  2 tbsp cider vinegar or lime juice
  3 tbsp cilantro or parsley, finely chopped
  2 clove garlic, minced
  ¾ tsp cumin powder
  ½ tsp salt
  black pepper to taste

Gently toss together.

FRUIT SALSA

Phase 1

✦ *Combine in a bowl:*
  ½ large grapefruit, sectioned and diced
  2 tbsp red onion, finely chopped
  ⅛ tsp hot pepper flakes
  1 tsp honey
  1 tbsp lemon juice
  1 cup fresh or thawed blueberries
  2 tbsp cilantro, chopped

Mix gently, then serve immediately.

Fruit salsa is great over fish or chicken.

Big Batch Tomato Salsa

THAI PEANUT SAUCE

Phase 1

✦ *In a saucepan, combine:*
   ¼ cup light peanut butter
   ¼ cup light soy sauce
   2 tbsp lemon juice
   2 tsp sesame seed oil
   2 tsp fresh ginger, grated
   1 tbsp honey
   1 tsp garlic powder
   pinch of hot pepper flakes

Heat over medium heat until bubbling, stirring constantly. Remove from heat and let cool. Store in fridge.

For a quick dinner, pour Thai Peanut Sauce over cooked chicken and place under broiler for 5 to 7 minutes. Serve with vegetables.

FAST VEGGIE DIP

Phase 1

✦ *Combine in a bowl:*
   2 cups low-fat sour cream
   ½ package onion soup mix
   ¼ cup low-fat mayonnaise

Makes a great dip for vegetables and pita chips, and as a spread in pitas and wraps.

MINT YOGURT DIP

Phase 1

✦ *In a medium size bowl, mix:*
   ½ clove garlic, minced
   2 cups low-fat plain yogurt
   2 tbsp fresh mint (or 1 tbsp dried mint)

Serve with a platter of fresh vegetables.

DIP WITH A TWIST

Phase 1

✦ *Combine in a bowl:*
   1 cup low-fat vanilla yogurt
   1 tsp dried dill
   ¼ tsp garlic powder

Makes a vegetable dip that combines a sweet flavour with a garlic "twist."

FRUIT DIP

Phase 1

✦ *Combine in a bowl:*
   1 cup low-fat vanilla yogurt
   1 tsp cinnamon
   ¼ tsp nutmeg

Makes a unique dip for assorted fresh fruits!

TZATZIKI SAUCE

Phase 1

✦ *Combine in a bowl:*
   1¼ cup low-fat plain yogurt
   ¼ cup low-fat mayonnaise
   juice of 1 lemon (¼ cup)
   3 cloves garlic, minced
   ½ tsp salt
✦ *Add:*
   1 cucumber, peeled, seeded and diced then
      patted dry with a paper towel
   salt and pepper to taste

Nutrition Tip
Garlic contains powerful immune supporting, cancer-fighting and heart health properties. When used in cooking, more that 70 sulphur-bearing compounds are released. The compounds hinder cancer cell growth and have antiviral, antibacterial and antifungal properties.

HUMMUS

Phase 1

✦ *With a food processor or hand mixer, combine:*

1 can (19 oz/540 ml) chickpeas, drained
2 green onions, chopped
3 cloves garlic, chopped
¼ cup fresh lemon juice (juice of one lemon)
¼ cup peanut butter or tahini (sesame seed paste)
½ cup low-fat plain yogurt
½ tsp ground cumin
½ tsp salt
pepper to taste

Blend well. Serve chilled or at room temperature with raw vegetables and pita bread. Garnish with chopped onions, tomato, or parsley.

LIGHT TARTAR SAUCE

Phase 1

✦ *Stir together in a small bowl:*

½ cup plain yogurt
⅓ cup low-fat mayonnaise
3 tbsp dill pickle, chopped
1 tsp lemon juice
½ tsp dijon mustard
dash hot pepper sauce
dash Worcestershire sauce

Cover and refrigerate. Serve with fish or on fish burgers.

This sauce can be stored in a well-sealed container or jar up to 5 days.

Hummus

Flaxseed Pancakes

30 Minute Solutions

30 Minute Solutions

The following recipes require a little more time to prepare, but are well worth the effort. Each section is packed with a variety of nutritious, low-glycemic meals. There is something to please the palate of every member of the family. Categories include brunch ideas, soups, salads and dressings, as well as main meals, meatless meals and side dishes. And last but not least, there are always the finishing touches of a few desserts and snack ideas.

Flaxseed Pancakes

Phase 2 • Makes 4 servings (12 pancakes)

1¼ cup	whole wheat flour
½ cup	ground flaxseed
1 tbsp	cinnamon
1 tbsp	sugar
1 tbsp	baking powder
1¾ cup	skim milk
1	egg
1 tsp	vanilla extract

1. In a large bowl, mix whole wheat flour, ground flaxseed, cinnamon, sugar, and baking powder. Set aside.

2. In a medium bowl, whisk together skim milk, egg and vanilla. Pour wet mixture into flour mixture and stir until combined.

3. Heat a large non-stick frying pan over medium-high heat. Spray with oil before spooning batter into pan. Reduce heat to medium-low. When tiny bubbles appear on top side of pancake, flip and cook for approximately 2 more minutes or until golden and cooked through.

4. Serve with toppings such as fresh fruit, no-sugar jams, or 1 tsp peanut butter or almond butter.

In order to release the oil in flaxseed, it is necessary to grind the seeds into flax meal. All it takes is a few seconds in a coffee grinder.

Nutrition Tip

Flaxseed is one of the best sources of omega-3 fat, fibre and lignans. Lignans are plant compounds with hormone-like activity (also referred to as phytoestrogens). They are especially important in the fight against hormone-sensitive cancers like breast and prostate cancer. Regular consumption of flaxseed has been associated with reduction of total cholesterol and LDL (bad) cholesterol levels. Aim to add ground flaxseed to your diet on a regular basis.

Brunch

Hearty Oatmeal Pancakes

Phase 2 • Makes 4 to 6 servings

½ cup	slow cook oats
½ cup	low-fat plain yogurt
½ cup	skim milk
2	large eggs
1 tbsp	canola oil
2 tbsp	brown sugar, packed
½ tsp	salt
1 tsp	baking powder
1 cup	whole wheat flour

1. In a medium bowl, combine oats, yogurt and milk. Set aside for 15 to 20 minutes to let the oats soften.

2. When the oats are finished soaking, beat in the egg and oil; mix well. Add the sugar and salt, then baking powder and flour. Stir until just moistened. For best results, let the batter stand for 5 minutes before cooking.

3. Heat a lightly oiled or non-stick griddle over medium heat (375°F for an electric frying pan).

4. For each pancake, pour about ¼ cup batter onto the griddle. Turn when the tops are covered with bubbles and look dry.

5. Serve with applesauce or yogurt.

Egg and Tofu Scramble

Phase 1 • Makes 2 to 3 servings

2	eggs
1 pkg (350 g)	extra firm tofu, crumbled
½	medium white onion, finely chopped
½	red bell pepper, diced
1 cup	mushrooms, chopped
¼ tsp	turmeric
½ tsp	salt

1. Beat eggs with tofu, set aside.

2. Sauté onion, pepper and mushrooms in a large non-stick frying pan over medium heat.

3. Add egg/tofu mixture, turmeric and salt. Stir until cooked.

4. Serve with salsa.

About Tofu

Tofu, made from the milk of soybeans, is a versatile, convenient food that can be made into a meal in minutes. It can be scrambled, stir-fried, baked, or added to soups, stews, shakes, lasagna and burritos. Tofu can be purchased in extra firm, firm, medium firm, medium soft or silken textures. Read the labels and purchase a variety with added calcium. Many food products are made from tofu, including soy cheese and meat substitutes.

COOKING TOFU

• Drain excess water from tofu before using it. For medium firm tofu, let it sit in a colander for 10 minutes or pat dry with a paper towel before using.

• Always cook tofu over low heat and do not over-cook it. Over-cooking causes tofu to become dry and tough.

• Marinate tofu in a glass or enamel dish; a metal dish may leave an unpleasant taste.

STORING TOFU

After tofu is opened, store the unused portion in the fridge immersed in water, where it will stay fresh for three to four days. Tofu is perishable and must be kept refrigerated.

BENEFITS OF SOYBEANS

The soybean has a unique composition offering a good balance of nutrients including high quality protein, fiber and essential fatty acids such as omega-3. Soybeans are often referred to as the best protein source originating from the soil. Soy is the only legume that contains a complete protein that is almost equivalent in quality to the protein found in dairy and meat products. Soy also contains isoflavones that may provide protection against heart disease, certain forms of cancer and osteoporosis.

Bean Burritos

Phase 2 • Makes 4 servings

1 tbsp	olive oil
½ cup	onion, finely chopped
1 clove	garlic, finely chopped
½ tsp	ground cumin
½ tsp	chili powder
1 can (19 oz/540 ml)	kidney beans, drained and mashed
1 tbsp	vinegar
to taste	salt (if desired)
4	whole wheat or sprouted grain tortillas (8-inch)

1. Heat oil in non-stick frying pan. Add onion and garlic and sauté until softened.

2. While stirring over medium heat, add cumin, chili powder, mashed beans and vinegar. Cook until heated through.

3. Divide bean mixture evenly among 4 tortillas.

4. Top with the following items:
   - a small amount of low-fat grated cheddar cheese
   - salsa
   - low-fat sour cream
   - tomatoes
   - shredded lettuce

5. Roll up and serve.

Bean Burrito

Egg Tortilla Bowls

Phase 2 • Makes 6 servings

8	eggs
2	green onions, chopped
½ cup	red bell pepper, chopped
⅓ cup	skim milk
to taste	salt and pepper
6	whole wheat tortillas (small, 6 to 8 inches)
⅓ cup	low-fat cheddar cheese, grated

1. Preheat oven to 375°F.

2. In a medium size bowl, whisk together eggs, green onions, red pepper, skim milk, salt and pepper.

3. Place tortillas into deep muffin tins or small oven-safe bowls (one per bowl). Pour egg mixture into tortillas. Sprinkle with cheddar cheese.

4. Bake 30 minutes or until centre is set. Let sit for approximately 5 minutes before serving.

Option: Add ½ cup salsa to eggs rather than green onions and red bell pepper.

Bake in fluted baking pans to dress up this dish.

Nutrition Tip

Flax, whole wheat or sprouted wheat tortillas make a lower glycemic alternative to traditional breads.

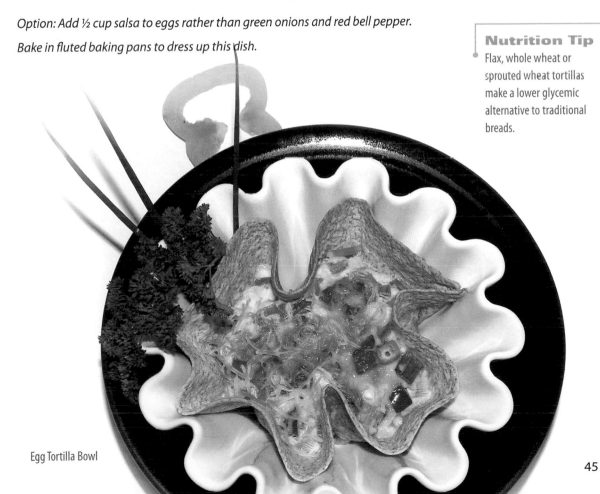

Egg Tortilla Bowl

Amazing Quiche

Phase 2 • Makes 4 to 6 servings

4	large eggs
1½ cups	1% milk
¼ cup	whole wheat flour
3 tbsp	cornmeal
3	green onions, chopped
½	red bell pepper, finely chopped
1 cup	low-fat cheddar cheese, grated
½ tsp	salt
½ tsp	black pepper

1. Preheat oven to 400°F. Spray a 9-inch pie plate with vegetable oil.

2. In a blender or food processor, combine eggs, milk, flour and cornmeal. Blend for 30 seconds, until well blended.

3. In the prepared pie plate, gently toss green onions, red pepper, grated cheese, salt and pepper. Pour the milk and egg mixture over the cheese mixture.

4. Bake 30 minutes, or until a knife inserted in the center comes out clean.

Nutrition Tip

Adequate intake of both calcium and vitamin D can reduce the risk of developing osteoporosis. Both children and adults need 1000 to 1500 mg of calcium daily, depending on age. In terms of food, that means consuming at least 3 servings of milk products every day. One serving includes 1 cup milk or enriched soy milk, ¾ cup yogurt, or 1½ oz cheese. Most people can't get enough calcium and vitamin D in their diets, so we recommend a pharmaceutical grade calcium supplement containing magnesium and vitamin D.

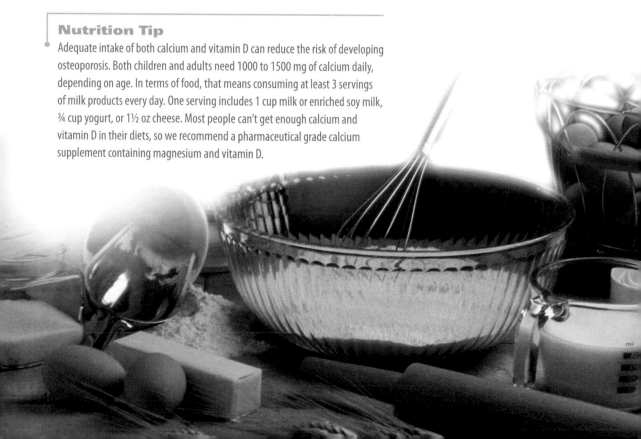

Homemade Turkey Sausage Patties

Phase 1 • Makes 8 to 10 patties

½ cup	slow cook oats
¼ cup	minced onion
1½ tbsp	dried parsley
1½ tsp	salt
1 tsp	black pepper, freshly ground
1 tsp	dried sage
½ tsp	ground cloves
½ tsp	ground nutmeg
2	eggs
1 pound	lean ground turkey

1. In a small bowl, combine oats, onion, parsley, salt, pepper, sage, cloves and nutmeg.

2. In a medium bowl, beat egg with a fork. Add turkey and oats mixture; mix well. Shape into 4 to 6 patties about ½ inch thick.

3. Preheat frying pan over medium heat. Place patties in preheated pan and cook for 5 minutes. Flip and continue cooking for 5 to 7 minutes, or until no longer pink inside.

Homemade Turkey Sausage Patties

Nutrition Tip

Ground turkey and chicken are lower-fat alternatives to ground beef. For food safety, ensure that the ground meat is cooked throughout and is no longer pink, or until food thermometer registers 165°F or 71°C .

Brunch

Minestrone Soup

Phase 2 • Makes 8 servings

1 tbsp	olive oil
1	large onion, chopped
3	medium carrots, sliced
2 stalks	celery, sliced
1 cup	cabbage, chopped
1	red potato, peeled and diced
3 cloves	garlic, finely chopped
1 can (19 oz/540 ml)	kidney or romano beans
1 can (28 oz/796 ml)	tomatoes
6 cups	water or beef broth
1 tsp	dried oregano
1 tsp	dried basil
½ cup	whole wheat macaroni, uncooked
to taste	salt and pepper
	parmesan cheese, grated

1. In a large pot, sauté onion, carrots, celery and garlic in the oil until tender.

2. Drain and rinse the beans.

3. Add the cabbage, potato, beans, tomatoes, water and oregano.

4. Bring to a boil; then reduce the heat. Cover and simmer for 30 minutes or until vegetables are tender.

5. Add the pasta. Cook over low heat for 15 minutes or until the pasta is tender.

6. Add salt, pepper or other seasonings if needed. Sprinkle with parmesan cheese before serving.

• *Rutabaga or zucchini can also be added to this soup.*

• *For added protein, add ½ pound of ground beef and sauté with the vegetables.*

• *To make beef, poultry or vegetable broth use commercial bouillon cubes, paste, or the low-sodium canned version. When using canned broth, dilute with ½ water to lower the sodium.*

Black Bean Soup

Phase 1 • Makes 6 to 8 servings

2 tbsp	vegetable oil
2 stalks	celery, chopped
1	large onion, chopped
3	medium carrots, chopped
3 cloves	garlic, finely chopped
1 tbsp	ground cumin
1 can (28 oz/796 ml)	diced tomatoes
6 cups	water
2 cans (19 oz/540 ml)	black beans, rinsed and drained
1 tsp	salt
¼ tsp	hot pepper flakes (or to taste)

1. In a large pot, sauté celery, onion, carrots and garlic in the oil until softened. Stir in cumin and sauté 1 minute longer.

2. Stir in the tomatoes, water and black beans. Bring to a boil, then reduce heat. Cover and simmer for 30 minutes.

3. Add salt and hot pepper flakes to taste.

4. Serve topped with a spoonful of plain yogurt or fresh salsa (optional).

This soup keeps up to 4 days in the fridge or 4 months in the freezer.

• Any 19 oz/540 ml can of beans can be used in place of black beans.

• To give a smoother texture, ladle out a portion of the soup and mash with a potato masher or purée in a blender or food processor, then stir back into the soup.

Black Bean Soup

Red Lentil Soup

Phase 1 • Makes 4 to 6 servings

1 cup	dried red lentils, rinsed and drained
2	onions, coarsely chopped
5 to 6 cups	water or vegetable stock
1	bay leaf
2 cloves	garlic, minced
1 tsp	dried thyme (or 1 tbsp fresh chopped)
3	carrots, sliced thinly
3 tbsp	fresh parsley, chopped
1 tsp	salt
to taste	pepper

1. In a large saucepan, combine lentils, onions, water, bay leaf and garlic. Cover and bring to a boil. Reduce heat and simmer for 20 minutes.

2. Add thyme and carrots. Simmer covered for 30 additional minutes or until carrots are tender and lentils are soft.

3. Remove bay leaf. Add parsley, salt and pepper to taste.

Red Lentil Soup

Split Pea Soup

Phase 1 • Makes 6 to 8 servings

1 tbsp	olive oil
1	onion, chopped
3	carrots, chopped
3 stalks	celery, chopped
2 cloves	garlic, minced
2 cups	green or yellow split peas or a mixture of both
½ tsp	dried thyme
4 cups	vegetable or chicken broth
3 cups	water
1 tsp	salt
1 tsp	black pepper

1. In a large pot, heat the oil over medium heat. Sauté onion, carrots, celery and garlic in the oil until softened.

2. Add the split peas, thyme and stock. Bring to a boil, then reduce heat. Cover and simmer for 1 to 1½ hours until the peas are tender.

3. Add salt, pepper and other seasonings as needed.

For Phase 2, add ½ cup barley and add more water if desired.

Pea soup is wonderful when flavoured with a ham bone. Make the broth ahead of time by simmering the ham bone in water, then cool and skim fat.

Nutrition Tip

Legumes (such as chickpeas, beans and lentils) are an excellent source of soluble dietary fiber which helps in the regulation of blood sugar and in lowering blood cholesterol levels. Other sources of soluble fiber include oat bran, oatmeal, brown rice, barley, and pectin rich fruits (apples, strawberries and citrus fruit).

Curried Sweet Potato and Cauliflower Soup

Phase 1 • Makes 4 to 6 servings

3 cups	sweet potato, chopped
2 cups	cauliflower, chopped
2 tsp	garlic, crushed
2 tsp	olive oil
1 cup	onion, chopped
1 tsp	curry powder
½ tsp	cinnamon
⅛ tsp	salt
4 cups	vegetable stock

1. Place sweet potato and cauliflower in a microwave-safe dish with ½ cup water. Cover and microwave for 8 to 10 minutes, or until vegetables are tender. Set aside.

2. Sauté garlic and onion in oil in a large stock pot over medium-high heat until softened.

3. Add curry, cinnamon, salt.

4. Combine onion and sweet potato/cauliflower mixture in a food processor and purée until creamy smooth.

5. Pour all ingredients back into the stock pot. Add vegetable stock and heat to desired temperature, adding additional stock if desired.

6. Garnish with cilantro and low-fat sour cream.

Orange Carrot Soup

Phase 1 • Makes 4 servings

2 tbsp	non-hydrogenated margarine
½ cup	onion, chopped
4 cups	carrots, sliced
4 cups	vegetable stock
½ cup	orange juice
½ tsp	nutmeg
¼ tsp	black pepper
1 cup	skim milk
¼ cup	low-fat sour cream (optional)

1. In a large stock pot, sauté onions in margarine over medium heat for 5 to 6 minutes until softened.

2. Add carrots and stock; bring to a boil. Reduce heat and simmer for 15 to 20 minutes. Stir in orange juice, nutmeg and pepper.

3. Transfer soup to a food processor or blender and purée until smooth.

4. Return soup to stock pot; stir in milk. Simmer over low heat for 2 to 3 minutes until heated through.

5. Stir in 1 tbsp sour cream per serving (optional).

Orange Carrot Soup

Soups

Creamy Roasted Vegetable Soup

Phase 1 • Makes 4 to 6 Servings

2 cups	squash, roasted *
1 cup	vegetables, roasted *
½ cup	water
4 cups	vegetable or beef broth
1 tsp	ground cumin
1 tsp	dried basil
1 tsp	dried oregano
1 tsp	salt

1. In a food processor, blend squash, roasted vegetables and water.

2. Pour contents into a large stock pot.

3. Add vegetable broth and spices. Bring to boil and simmer for 10 to 15 minutes.

* For roasting instructions see page 81.

Basic Salad and Dressings

Phase 1 • Makes 2 servings

1½ cups	salad greens (romaine, leaf, boston, spinach)
1	small carrot, grated
½ cup	red, yellow or green bell pepper, diced
1	plum tomato, cut into wedges
½ cup	cucumber, sliced
¼ cup	red onion, chopped

Toss above ingredients in a small bowl. Serve with 2 tablespoons of one of the following dressings or use your favourite low-fat dressing.

LOW-FAT DRESSINGS

ORANGE VINAIGRETTE

Makes 1 cup

2 cloves	garlic, crushed
¼ cup	fresh parsley, chopped (or 1 tbsp dry)
¼ cup	white vinegar
½ cup	orange juice
¼ cup	flax oil
2 tsp	sugar
½ tsp	salt

freshly ground pepper to taste

In a small jar or blender, add garlic, parsley, vinegar, orange juice, canola oil, sugar, salt and pepper to taste. Mix well.

YOGURT DILL DRESSING

Makes 2 cups

1½ cups	low-fat plain yogurt
¼ cup	low-fat mayonnaise
1 tbsp	white vinegar
1 tsp	dried dill weed (or 3 tbsp fresh)
⅓ cup	fresh parsley, chopped
1 tsp	dijon mustard
1 clove	garlic, minced

fresh ground pepper

In a small jar or bowl, combine all ingredients and whisk well. Covered and refrigerated, this dressing will keep up to a week.

Salads

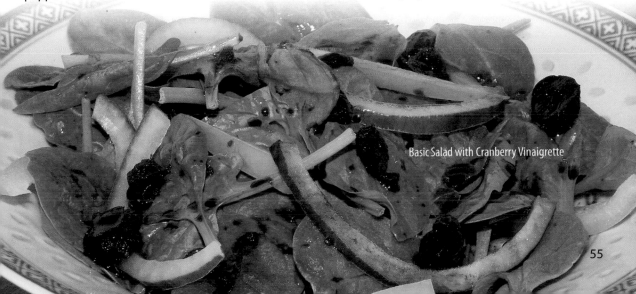

Basic Salad with Cranberry Vinaigrette

CRANBERRY VINAIGRETTE

Makes 2 cups

½ cup	dried cranberries
2 cloves	garlic, crushed
1 tbsp	olive oil
½ tsp	salt and pepper
½ cup	orange juice
¼ cup	balsamic vinegar
¼ cup	flaxseed oil (or olive oil)

In a frying pan, place cranberries, garlic, oil, salt and pepper and cook over medium heat. Stir constantly. When ingredients come to a boil, reduce heat and cook for 2 minutes. Transfer to a bowl. Add orange juice, balsamic vinegar and oil. Let cool while preparing salad. Pour over salad and toss well.

GINGER-SESAME DRESSING

Makes 1 cup

¼ cup	rice vinegar (or white vinegar)
¼ cup	orange juice
2 tbsp	low-sodium soy sauce
2 tbsp	peanut butter
1 tbsp	sesame oil
1 tbsp	brown sugar
1 tsp	garlic, crushed
2 tsp	fresh ginger, grated (or 1 tsp ground)

Combine all ingredients in a blender and purée until smooth. Chill 2 hours before serving.

All of these dressings are low-fat because the oil has been partially replaced by orange juice, low-fat yogurt or low-fat mayonnaise.

Yogurt Dill Dressing, Cranberry Vinaigrette, and Orange Vinaigrette

Basic Coleslaw

Phase 1 • Makes 4 to 6 servings

4 cups	cabbage, shredded (about half a medium cabbage)
2	medium carrots, grated
½ cup	onion, finely chopped

DRESSING

1 tbsp	flaxseed oil
3 tbsp	white vinegar
1 tsp	salt
1 tsp	sugar

1. In a medium bowl, combine cabbage, carrots and onion.

2. Dressing: In a small bowl or jar, mix together oil, vinegar, salt and sugar. Pour over salad.

Try the Orange Vinaigrette dressing on page 55 as a zesty alternative.

Salads

Basic Coleslaw

Broccoli Walnut Salad

Phase 1 • Makes 6 to 8 servings

1 head	fresh broccoli (about 1 pound)
1 cup	red onion, chopped
½ cup	dark raisins
½ cup	walnuts
1 cup	red seedless grapes

DRESSING

½ cup	low-fat mayonnaise
½ cup	low-fat sour cream
1 tbsp	honey
½ tsp	ground ginger

1. Peel the tough outer skin from the broccoli stalk and discard. Chop the stalks into ½ inch pieces and cut the tops into small florets. (There should be about 6 cups of broccoli florets and stems).

2. In a large bowl, combine broccoli, onions, raisins, and walnuts and toss well.

3. Dressing: In a small bowl, combine mayonnaise, sour cream, honey and ginger; stir to mix well. Add the dressing to the broccoli mixture and toss to mix.

4. Cover the salad and refrigerate for several hours or overnight before serving.

Nutrition Tip

Did you know? A handful of walnuts helps meet your daily requirement of omega-3 fatty acids. Eating a small handful each day will help to reduce the amount of LDL "bad" cholesterol in the blood. Walnuts are a source of protein, minerals, essential vitamins, and powerful antioxidants. Store walnuts in the refrigerator to avoid rancidity.

Colourful Black Bean and Corn Salad

Phase 2 • Makes 6 servings
This salad is best made at least 4 to 6 hours ahead of time to allow the flavours to blend.
It keeps well in the refrigerator for up to 3 days.

SALAD

1 can (19 oz/540 ml)	black beans, rinsed and drained
1 can (12 oz/341 ml)	corn kernels, drained
1	large tomato, diced
1	green bell pepper, diced
1	small red onion, finely chopped
2 tbsp	fresh cilantro, chopped

DRESSING

¼ cup	lime juice (juice of 1 lime)
2 tbsp	red wine vinegar
2 tbsp	flaxseed oil
1 tsp	ground cumin
½ tsp	hot pepper sauce (optional)
to taste	salt and pepper

1. In a large bowl, combine beans, corn, tomatoes, peppers, onions and cilantro. Set aside.

2. Dressing: In a small bowl or glass jar, whisk together lime juice, vinegar, oil, cumin, hot pepper sauce (if using), salt and pepper to taste.

3. Pour dressing over salad. Garnish with cilantro.

For a speedy dressing, add ½ tsp cumin to ¼ cup bottled oil and vinegar salad dressing.

Salads

Colourful Black Bean
and Corn Salad

Chicken Caesar Salad

Phase 2 (Phase 1 without the croutons) • Makes 4 to 6 servings

CAESAR DRESSING

¾ cup	1% cottage cheese
½ cup	skim milk
2	cloves garlic, minced
¼ cup	lemon juice, freshly squeezed (juice of one lemon)
1½ tsp	dijon mustard
1 tsp	Worcestershire sauce
½ tsp	salt
½ tsp	black pepper, freshly ground
1 tbsp	olive oil
¼ cup	parmesan cheese, freshly grated

QUICK CROUTONS

2	slices whole wheat bread
2 tsp	olive oil
½ tsp	garlic powder
¼ tsp each	dried oregano, basil and thyme

SALAD

8 cups	romaine lettuce, torn (about 2 medium heads)
¼ cup	parmesan cheese, freshly grated

CHICKEN

2 cups	cooked chicken, chopped

continued next page

1. Prepare the dressing: In a food processor or blender, purée cottage cheese until smooth. Blend in garlic, lemon juice, mustard, salt and pepper. Add olive oil and blend until thick and smooth. Add parmesan cheese and blend until just mixed. Cover and refrigerate for at least 1 hour or up to a day.

2. Prepare the croutons: Cut bread into cubes. In a glass pie plate, toss bread cubes with olive oil, garlic powder and Italian seasoning. Microwave, covered with a paper towel, on High, stopping twice to stir, for 3 to 4 minutes, or until crisp. Set aside to cool.

3. Prepare the salad: Place lettuce in a large salad bowl, pour in dressing and toss. Sprinkle with parmesan and croutons, toss lightly and serve immediately.

4. Top with cooked chicken (heated if desired).

Caesar salad must be eaten immediately after tossing or it goes limp. Prepare the lettuce ahead of time and keep it crisp in a plastic bag with a paper towel inside. Make the dressing ahead of time and keep it in the refrigerator until ready to toss with the salad.

Nutrition Tip

Olive oil is an excellent source of monounsaturated fat. This fat may help to lower the risk of heart disease because it reduces total cholesterol as well as the LDL "bad" cholesterol in the blood. Try replacing other fats such as butter or margarine with olive oil.

Salads

Chicken Caesar Salad

Big Batch Creamy Cole Slaw

Phase 1 • Makes 8 to 10 servings

½ cup	low-fat mayonnaise
½ cup	low-fat plain yogurt
2 tbsp	sugar or sweetener of choice
2	green onions, finely chopped
2 tsp	lemon juice
1 tbsp	white vinegar
1 tbsp	dijon mustard
¼ tsp	celery seed
¾ tsp	salt
¼ tsp	black pepper
5 cups	cabbage, shredded
3 cups	carrots, grated
½ cup	dried cranberries (optional)

1. In a large bowl, mix together mayonnaise, yogurt, sugar, onion, lemon juice, vinegar, mustard, celery seed, salt and pepper.

2. Add cabbage, carrots and cranberries. Stir well.

3. Chill 1 to 2 hours before serving.

Nutrition Tip

Many artificial sweeteners are much sweeter than sugar, therefore less is needed to sweeten foods. Splenda™ is the trade name for sucralose, one of the more prevalent artificial sweeteners. Many people with diabetes or those following a low-G.I. diet use artificial sweeteners because they do not affect blood sugar. If you have concerns about artificial sweeteners, you can find an excellent medical overview at www.fda.gov. If you prefer not to use artificial sweeteners, then fructose is a better alternative than sugar. The herbal sweetener, stevia, which can be found in health food stores is also a great choice.

Curried Chicken and Apple Salad

Phase 1 • Makes 6 servings
This is Cheryl's teenage son Aaron's favorite recipe!

1 tbsp	canola oil
1 tbsp	curry powder
⅓ cup	purple onion, diced
2 tbsp	lemon juice, fresh
2 tbsp	sugar or sweetener of choice
¼ tsp	salt
⅓ cup	low-fat mayonnaise
⅓ cup	low-fat plain yogurt
2	cooked chicken breasts, cubed
3 stalks	celery, thinly sliced
½ cup	red bell pepper, chopped
1	medium apple, cut in ¼-inch cubes
6	dried apricots, diced
	salad greens

1. Dressing: Heat oil in a small saucepan over medium-high heat. Add curry powder and onion. Sauté 1 to 2 minutes or until onions are tender. Add lemon juice, sugar and salt. Simmer over medium heat until sauce begins to thicken, about 1 minute. Remove from heat and cool. Stir mayonnaise and yogurt into cooled sauce; set aside.

2. In a large bowl, toss together chicken, celery, red pepper, apple and apricots. Add dressing and gently toss until evenly coated.

3. Serve chicken mixture on a bed of salad greens. Garnish with chopped apricots and red pepper, if desired.

Salads

Curried Chicken and Apple Salad

Tangy Beet Salad Ring

Phase 1 • Makes 6 servings
This tangy salad is a great complement to roast beef.

2 cans (14 oz/398 ml)	diced beets (or fresh beets, steamed and diced)
2 envelopes	unflavoured gelatin
⅔ cup	white vinegar
2 tbsp	horseradish
2 tbsp	sugar or sweetener of choice
	cottage cheese or plain yogurt (optional)

1. Drain beets, reserving juice.

2. Measure beet juice and add enough water to make 1½ cups of liquid. Pour into a medium size pot. Sprinkle gelatin into beet juice to soften. Stir over low heat until gelatin dissolves completely.

3. Add vinegar and horseradish, then add beets and sugar.

4. Pour into a small ring or mould and chill until firm. May be served with cottage cheese or yogurt.

Tangy Beet Salad Ring

Kidney Bean, Cabbage and Feta Salad

Phase 1 • Makes 6 servings

1 can (19 oz/540 ml)	red kidney beans, rinsed and drained
3 cups	cabbage, finely chopped
1	red bell pepper, chopped
2	green onions, chopped
½ cup	feta cheese, cubed
3 tbsp	fresh parsley, chopped

DRESSING

2 tbsp	lemon juice
1 tbsp	flaxseed oil
2	cloves garlic, minced
1 tsp	dried basil, optional

1. In a salad bowl, combine beans, cabbage, red pepper, onions, feta cheese and parsley.

2. In a jar with a tight fitting lid, combine dressing ingredients and shake.

3. Pour dressing over salad and toss lightly.

4. Cover and refrigerate until chilled.

Salads

Kidney Bean, Cabbage and Feta Salad

Lentil Rice Salad

Phase 2 • Makes 4 to 6 servings

½ cup	basmati rice
1 tbsp	olive oil
2	carrots, peeled, finely chopped
1	small onion, chopped
2 cloves	garlic, finely chopped
½ cup	dried green or brown lentils, rinsed and drained
1 cup	water or broth
1	red bell pepper, chopped

1. Cook rice according to package directions to yield 2 cups of cooked rice (½ cup raw).

2. Heat oil in a large saucepan. Add the carrot, onion and garlic and sauté until the onion is translucent, about 5 minutes. Stir in the lentils. Add water (or broth) and bring to a boil over high heat. Reduce heat and simmer for 20 to 25 minutes until lentils are tender but not mushy. Transfer the lentils to a large bowl.

3. Add red pepper and cooked rice to lentils. Toss with Lemon Basil Vinaigrette. Serve warm or chilled.

LEMON BASIL VINAIGRETTE

2 tbsp	flaxseed oil or olive oil
1 tsp	lemon rind, finely grated
¼ cup	lemon juice, freshly squeezed (juice of one lemon)
1½ tsp	fresh basil or ½ tsp dried basil
¼ tsp	salt

In a screw-top jar combine flaxseed oil, lemon rind, lemon juice, basil and salt. Cover and shake well.

Lentil Rice Salad

Mixed Bean Salad

Phase 1 • Makes 6 servings
Packed with fiber, this low-glycemic salad is perfect for lunch.

1 cup	green beans or 1 can (10 oz/284 ml), drained
1 cup	yellow beans or 1 can (10 oz/284 ml), drained
1 can (19 oz/540 ml)	chickpeas, drained
1 can (19 oz/540 ml)	red kidney beans, drained
1	small red bell pepper, chopped
½ cup	red onion, diced
¼ cup	fresh parsley, chopped
2 cups	romaine lettuce, shredded (optional)
2 cups	baby spinach leaves (optional)

DRESSING

⅓ cup	red wine vinegar
2 tbsp	flaxseed oil
1 tsp	sugar
2 cloves	garlic, minced
1 tbsp	Dijon mustard
2 tsp	celery seed
¼ tsp each	salt and pepper

Nutrition Tip
Green beans are packed with nutrients! They are a great source of fat-soluble vitamins (A, C, K), dietary fibre, potassium, folate, manganese, iron, and a number of other minerals.

Salads

1. If fresh green or yellow beans are being used, steam for about 5 minutes until tender crisp. Rinse under cold water until cool. Drain well. Cut in 1 inch pieces.

2. In a large bowl, combine steamed beans, canned beans, red pepper, onion and parsley.

3. To make dressing, combine red wine vinegar, flaxseed oil, garlic, dijon mustard, celery seed, salt and pepper in a jar with a tight lid. Shake well.

4. Pour over salad and toss gently.

5. Combine romaine and spinach and divide among 4 plates. Spoon bean mixture over greens to serve.

Mixed Bean Salad

Tabouli

Phase 1 • Makes 6 servings

Tastiest when fresh mint is available. Bulgur wheat is now universally available in bulk or prepackaged at your local grocery store. Add more vegetables as desired

1 cup	bulgur wheat
2 cups	boiling water
1 can (19 oz/540 ml)	chickpeas, drained and rinsed
1 cup	fresh parsley, chopped
½ cup	fresh mint, chopped
2	green onions, chopped
1 or 2	medium tomatoes, cut into small pieces

DRESSING

2 tbsp	flaxseed oil
1	lemon, juice and grated rind
1 tsp	salt
to taste	pepper

1. Measure bulgur wheat into a bowl and cover with boiling water. Let stand for ½ hour until all the water has been absorbed. Drain any excess and pat dry with a paper towel if necessary.

2. Stir chickpeas, parsley, mint, onions and tomatoes into bulgur.

3. Dressing: In a small bowl, whisk oil, lemon juice, lemon rind, salt and pepper. Pour over salad and mix well.

4. Chill for at least one hour before serving.

Covered and chilled, this dish will keep up to 4 days.

Colene's Spicy Carrot and Chickpea Salad

Phase 1 • Makes 6 servings

⅓ cup	low-fat plain yogurt
2 tbsp	olive oil
2 tbsp	lemon juice
½ tsp	sugar
1 tsp	ground cumin
½ tsp	ground coriander
¼ tsp each	salt and pepper
pinch	cinnamon and ginger
4 cups	carrots, grated
1 can (19 oz/540 ml)	chickpeas, rinsed and drained
2 tbsp	raisins or currants
2 tbsp	parsley, chopped
2 tbsp	fresh cilantro

Nutrition Tip

When choosing vegetables think orange, green and red. The colour is a reflection of its content of beta-carotene, a powerful antioxidant that protects against free radical damage. Carrots, broccoli, sweet potato, winter squash, and spinach are excellent sources of beta-carotene.

Salads

1. In a medium sized bowl, combine yogurt, oil, sugar, cumin, coriander, salt, pepper, cinnamon and ginger and mix well.

2. Add carrots, chickpeas, raisins, parsley and cilantro. Mix well.

3. Chill well before serving.

Colene's Spicy Carrot and Chickpea Salad

Quinoa and Black Bean Salad

Phase 2 • Makes 6 to 8 servings

1 cup	quinoa
1½ cups	water
2 tbsp	olive oil
1 tsp	paprika
1	large onion, finely chopped (2 cups)
2 cloves	garlic, minced
1 tsp	ground cumin
1 tsp	ground coriander
2	red bell peppers, diced
¼ tsp	hot pepper flakes
1 tbsp	cilantro, chopped
1 can (12 oz/341 ml)	corn, drained
1 can (14 oz/398 ml)	black beans, drained
1	large tomato, diced
½ cup	feta cheese, crumbled
1 small can	black olives (optional)
½ cup	pine nuts, toasted (optional)
¼ cup	lemon juice, freshly squeezed (juice of one lemon)
to taste	salt and pepper

1. In a sieve, rinse the quinoa under running water and drain.

2. Heat 1 tbsp oil in a saucepan. Add paprika and stir constantly for 1 minute. Add quinoa and water. Cover and bring to a boil. Lower heat and simmer 15 to 20 minutes, or until the water is absorbed and quinoa is tender, yet a bit chewy. If you prefer quinoa with a firmer texture, use 1 cup of water.

3. Heat 1 tbsp oil in a frying pan. Sauté onion, garlic, cumin and coriander until onions are translucent. Stir in red bell peppers, hot pepper flakes and cilantro. Sauté another 5 minutes.

4. Add cooked quinoa to sautéed vegetables. Stir in the corn, black beans, tomato, feta, olives, pine nuts, lemon juice, salt and pepper. Transfer to a bowl and refrigerate until ready to serve.

Greek Style Bulgur Salad

Phase 2 • Makes 4 to 6 servings

1 cup	bulgur wheat
2 cups	water
½	red onion, cut into rings
1	tomato, seeded and diced
1	green pepper, chopped
1	small zucchini, thinly sliced
½ cup	feta cheese
¼ cup	white wine vinegar
2 tbsp	flaxseed or olive oil
1 clove	garlic, minced
1 tsp	dried basil
1 tsp	dried oregano
1 tsp	salt
to taste	pepper

Salads

1. Boil water. Pour over bulgur and let stand for 30 minutes. Drain any excess water.

2. In a medium bowl, combine bulgur, onion, tomato, zucchini and feta cheese.

3. In a separate bowl, combine vinegar, oil, garlic, basil, oregano, salt and pepper. Cover and refrigerate to allow flavours to develop.

To make this a Phase 1 recipe, eliminate the bulgur.

Spaghetti Squash au Gratin

Main Meals

Szechuan Orange Ginger Chicken

Phase 1 • Makes 3 to 4 servings

1	orange, juice and grated rind
2 cloves	garlic, finely chopped
1 tbsp	fresh ginger, finely chopped
1 tbsp	cider vinegar
½ tsp	hot pepper sauce
1 tsp	sugar
1 tsp	cornstarch
3	chicken breasts
1	green bell pepper, cut into thin 1-inch strips
1	red bell pepper, cut into thin 1-inch strips
2 tbsp	vegetable oil

Nutrition Tip

Getting enough protein is critical for maintaining lean body mass, muscular strength, and a strong immune system. In addition to meat sources, choose protein-rich alternatives like dried beans, lentils, soy foods, and eggs more often. Including a protein at each meal and snack, will help control blood sugar, stave off hunger and keep you feeling full and satisfied.

1. Mix orange rind with chopped garlic and ginger and set aside.

2. Squeeze juice from orange and whisk together with vinegar, hot pepper sauce, sugar and cornstarch. Set aside.

3. Remove skin and bone from the chicken and slice into thin strips.

4. In a wok or large frying pan, heat the oil over medium-high heat. Cook the chicken in the hot oil for 3 to 4 minutes until cooked through or no longer pink inside. Remove and set aside.

5. Cook the ginger and garlic in the hot oil for 10 seconds. Add the bell peppers and stir-fry for 2 to 3 minutes.

6. Return the chicken and sauce to the stir-fry and cook until thickened.

For Phase 2, serve over cooked rice.

Main Meals

West Coast Teriyaki Salmon with Wasabi Mayonnaise

Phase 1 • Makes 4 servings

4	salmon fillets (4 oz/125g each), skinless and boneless
½ cup	teriyaki marinade (recipe below) or store-bought equivalent
½ cup	sesame seeds, toasted

TERIYAKI MARINADE

½ cup	orange juice
3 tbsp	low-sodium soy sauce
2 tbsp	brown sugar
2 cloves	garlic, chopped
1½ tbsp	ground ginger (or 2 tsp fresh ginger, grated)

WASABI MAYONNAISE

1 tsp	water
½ tbsp	wasabi powder
¼ cup	low-fat mayonnaise
1 tbsp	onion, finely chopped

1. Rinse fish and place in shallow dish, coat with teriyaki sauce; set aside.

2. Preheat oven to 400°F.

3. In a small bowl, combine wasabi powder and water to create a paste. Let sit 1 minute, then combine with mayonnaise.

4. Remove salmon from marinade and discard marinade. Coat top and sides of fish with toasted sesame seeds. Place on a lightly oiled cookie sheet. Barbecue or bake for 15 minutes until fish is opaque and cooked through.

5. Serve with Wasabi Mayonnaise.

West Coast Teriyaki Salmon

"Old Fashioned" Hearty Beef Stew

Phase 2 • Makes 8 servings

2 tbsp	olive oil
2 lbs	stewing beef, cut into ½ inch cubes
2 cloves	garlic, minced
2	medium onions, chopped
2 cups	beef stock
3	medium carrots, peeled and cut in ¼ inch coins
3 stalks	celery, chopped
3	small red potatoes, peeled and sliced
1 can (19 oz/540 ml)	diced tomatoes with juice
1	bay leaf
1 tbsp	Worcestershire sauce
¼ cup	fresh parsley (or 2 tbsp dried)
1 cup	frozen peas
to taste	salt and pepper

Nutrition Tip

The richest sources of iron are from beef, poultry, pork and lamb. The type of iron in these sources can be absorbed most efficiently by the body. Iron from plant foods such as dried fruit, whole grains, leafy green vegetables, nuts, seeds and legumes are not well absorbed by the body. To improve their absorption, add a source of vitamin C to your meal, for example, spinach salad tossed with orange segments.

1. Heat oil in a large frying pan over medium heat. Add beef, garlic and onions and brown for about 5 minutes. Remove from heat and place mixture in a slow cooker.

2. Add stock, carrots, celery, potatoes, tomatoes (with juice), bay leaf, Worcestershire sauce and parsley; stir to combine. Cover and cook on Low for 8 to 10 hours or on high for 4 to 6 hours, until vegetables are tender and stew is bubbling. Remove bay leaf and discard.

3. Add peas 20 minutes before serving. Cook on high until slightly thickened and peas are heated through. Season to taste with salt and pepper.

Main Meals

"Old Fashioned" Hearty Beef Stew

Halibut in White Wine

Phase 1 • Makes 6 to 9 servings

2 pounds/900 grams	halibut fillets, de-boned and skinned
⅓ cup	whole wheat flour
¼ tsp	salt
¼ tsp	black pepper, freshly ground
2 tbsp	olive oil
1	large onion, finely chopped
1	large carrot, finely chopped
¾ cup	white wine, vegetable stock or chicken stock
1 tbsp	dried parsley or a few sprigs of fresh

1. Preheat oven to 375°F.

2. Wash halibut in cool water and pat dry.

3. Combine flour, salt and pepper in large bowl. Dredge all sides of halibut in flour mixture and set aside.

4. Heat 1 tbsp of the oil in a large frying pan. Brown halibut fillets on both sides, approximately 4 minutes per side. Place in oven proof dish.

5. Heat 1 tbsp of the oil in frying pan and sauté carrots and onions for about 5 minutes. Add wine or stock and simmer for another 5 minutes. Pour over fish. Sprinkle with freshly ground pepper.

6. Bake 25 minutes. Serve garnished with parsley.

Halibut in White Wine

Beef and Broccoli Stir-Fry

Phase 1 • Makes 4 servings

¾ pound/300 grams	beef, thinly sliced (use round or sirloin)
2 to 3 cups	broccoli, cut into bite-sized pieces
1 to 2 tbsp	oil
1 tbsp	fresh ginger, finely chopped
3 cloves	garlic, finely chopped

MARINADE

1 tbsp	soy sauce
1 tsp	water
1 tsp	sesame oil (optional)

SAUCE

⅓ cup	stock or water
1 to 2 tbsp	soy sauce
½ tsp	sugar
1 tbsp	cornstarch

Nutrition Tip

Milk products are not the only source of calcium. Broccoli is a source of calcium, as are beans, tofu, kale, sesame seeds, almonds, canned fish, and fortified rice and soy beverages.

1. Marinade: Whisk together the sauce, water and sesame oil. Toss with beef strips to coat. Refrigerate.

2. Sauce: Whisk together stock, soy sauce, sugar and cornstarch. Set aside.

3. In a wok or large frying pan, heat the oil over medium-high heat. Swirl gently to coat the sides of the pan. Cook the ginger and garlic in hot oil for 10 seconds.

4. Add the beef and stir-fry 2 to 3 minutes until almost cooked through. Add broccoli and continue to stir-fry for 5 to 7 minutes.

5. Add the sauce and continue to stir-fry until thickened.

Main Meals

Fish Fillets on Spinach

Phase 1 • Makes 6 servings

1½ pounds/600 grams	fish fillets (approximately 6 fillets)
¼ cup	lemon juice (juice of one lemon)
6 cups	fresh spinach
2 tbsp	olive oil
1	medium onion, chopped
1 tsp	salt
¼ tsp	black pepper
½ tsp	nutmeg
2	tomatoes, sliced
¼ cup	low-fat mozzarella cheese, grated

1. Preheat oven to 350°F.

2. Wash fish, pat dry. Sprinkle with lemon juice and let stand 10 minutes.

3. Heat oil in frying pan. Add onion and sauté until soft. Fry fish in pan with onions for a few minutes on each side until browned. Remove from frying pan and set aside.

4. Add spinach to frying pan and stir-fry 4 to 5 minutes.

5. Lightly oil a casserole dish and place spinach on the bottom. Arrange fillets on top of spinach. Place sliced tomatoes on top of fillets. Sprinkle salt, pepper, and nutmeg on tomato slices. Top with cheese.

6. Bake 15 minutes.

Fish Fillets on Spinach

Kidney Bean Curry (Raj Mah Di Dal)

Phase 2 • Makes 4 servings
Thanks to Meena, our friend and associate, for this authentic Indian recipe.

2 tbsp	olive oil
1	small onion, chopped
4 cloves	garlic, diced
3 tsp	fresh ginger, diced
½ tsp	salt
1 tbsp	turmeric powder
½ tsp	ground coriander
to taste	cayenne pepper
1 can (19 oz/540 ml)	kidney beans
½ can	water
2 cups	cooked basmati rice

Nutrition Tip

Kidney beans are an excellent source of both soluble and insoluble fiber, containing 6 grams per ½ cup serving. Most people get only half of the 25 to 30 grams of fiber they need daily. Children need an amount of fiber that equals their age plus 5 grams.

1. Sauté onions in olive oil until slightly brown.

2. Add garlic and ginger and continue to sauté until browned.

3. Add salt, cayenne, turmeric, coriander, kidney beans and water. Bring to a boil and cook 10 to 12 minutes.

4. Serve over rice.

Meatless

Spaghetti Squash au Gratin

Phase 1 • Makes 4 to 6 servings

1	medium to large spaghetti squash
½ cup	parmesan cheese, grated
½ cup	mozzarella cheese, grated
⅓ cup	fresh parsley, chopped
1 tsp	oregano
2	Italian plum tomatoes, chopped

1. Pierce spaghetti squash several times with a fork or sharp knife (this will allow steam to escape during cooking). Microwave 10 to 12 minutes on high until shell is just soft, turning over half way through cooking. Remove and cool.

2. Preheat oven to 375°F.

3. Cut squash in half; remove and discard seeds. Use a fork to scrape insides of squash into a mixing bowl and separate strands. Reserve squash shells.

4. Toss squash strands and remaining ingredients together and spoon back into squash shell.

5. Bake 10 minutes or until lightly browned.

Spaghetti Squash au Gratin

Roasted Vegetables

Phase 1 • Makes 6 servings

5	large carrots, sliced into fries
3	sweet potatoes, sliced into fries
2	red bell peppers, quartered
1	large sweet onion, quartered
3 cloves	garlic, peeled
1 tsp	oregano
½ tsp each	salt and pepper
2 tbsp	olive oil

1. Position racks in top and bottom thirds of oven. Preheat to 450°F.

2. Place two large rimmed baking sheets in oven while preheating.*

3. Place all ingredients in a large bowl and toss until vegetables are evenly coated with oil.

4. Remove baking sheets from oven and tumble vegetables onto sheets and spread out.

5. Roast 25 to 35 minutes, switching trays half way through roasting.

* Heating baking sheets before adding vegetables seals in the flavour and helps vegetables develop a golden colour.

Roasted vegetables can be eaten as a side dish or used in Creamy Roasted Vegetable Soup on page 54.

Meatless

Roasted Winter Squash

Includes thick-skinned squashes such as acorn, hubbard, butternut, and pumpkin.

1. Preheat oven to 375°F.

2. Cut favorite squash in half, remove seeds.

3. Oil bottom of a roasting pan with 1 tablespoon of olive oil and place halved squash face down. Cover with a lid.

4. Bake 40 to 60 minutes or until the squash is tender. Remove skin after baking.

Barley Mushroom Pilaf

Phase 2 • Makes 6 to 8 servings

½ cup	fresh mushrooms, sliced
2 tsp	olive oil
1 cup	pearl barley
3 cups	beef broth
2	green onions, chopped
¼ tsp	ground savory
2 tbsp	parmesan cheese, grated

1. Heat olive oil in a saucepan; add mushrooms and sauté until soft.

2. Add barley, broth, green onion and savory. Bring to a boil. Reduce heat to low; cover and cook 45 minutes or until barley is tender and liquid is absorbed.

3. Sprinkle parmesan cheese over pilaf and serve.

Nutrition Tip

Barley is a chewy, versatile grain that is wonderful in soups and stews. It is one of the creamiest of all grains, and makes a delicious creamy pudding similar to rice pudding. Pot barley has only the outer husk removed. Pearl barley has had the bran removed and has been steamed and polished. Barley has a low glycemic index and can be used instead of rice.

Quinoa Pilaf

Phase 1 • Makes 6 servings

1 cup	quinoa
1½ cups	water
2 tbsp	olive oil
2 cloves	garlic, crushed
2 to 3 cups	vegetables, sliced (celery, green onion, green and red bell pepper, carrots, broccoli, cauliflower or zucchini)
2 tbsp	soy sauce or seasonings of choice (i.e. oregano, basil)
½ cup	toasted almonds (optional)

1. In a sieve, rinse quinoa under running water and drain.

2. In a medium saucepan or rice cooker, add water and quinoa. Cover and bring to a boil. Reduce heat and simmer 15 minutes or until tender. Use less water (1 cup) if you prefer quinoa with a firmer, chewier texture.

3. In a non-stick frying pan over medium heat, sauté garlic then stir-fry vegetables for about 4 minutes until tender crisp. Add cooked quinoa to vegetables. Add soy sauce or choice of seasonings.

4. Serve sprinkled with toasted almonds if desired.

Nutrition Tip

Quinoa (pronounced keen-wa) is a gluten free, low-glycemic grain with ancient origins. It comes from the Andes Mountains of South America, and was a staple in the Inca civilization. Quinoa is higher in protein than any other grain and a glycemic index of 35 makes it a great staple in your pantry. Quinoa is versatile, quick to prepare, and can be substituted for almost any grain in most recipes. Include generous amounts of grains in your diet and experiment with new ones, such as quinoa, bulgur, and buckwheat.

Meatless

Anya's Chickpea Burgers

Phase 1 • Makes 4 to 6 servings
Laura's daughter Anya, who has type 1 diabetes, loves these low-glycemic burgers.
Makes a great after school snack.

1 tbsp	olive oil
1	large onion, finely chopped
2 cloves	garlic, minced
1 can (19 oz/540 ml)	chickpeas, rinsed and drained
1 cup	whole grain bread crumbs, loosely packed
1	egg
¼ cup	flaxseed, ground
1 tsp	ground cumin
¼ tsp	salt
½ tbsp	dried parsley
pinch	cayenne pepper
1 to 2 tbsp	whole wheat flour (optional)

1. Heat oil in a frying pan. Add onion and garlic and cook over low heat for 5 minutes or until golden.

2. In a food processor, purée chickpeas until they resemble bread crumbs. Add bread crumbs, flaxseed, cumin, salt, parsley, and pepper. Process for a few seconds.

3. Add onion and garlic mixture to ingredients in food processor. Process until just combined. Add whole wheat flour if mixture is too wet to form patties.

4. Form into patties.

5. Spray a non-stick frying pan with cooking spray and fry patties over medium heat until browned, approximately 4 minutes per side.

Delicious served with Greek salad.

Nutrition Tip

The chickpea, a legume also known as the garbanzo bean, is popular in Middle Eastern and Mediterranean dishes, including hummus and falafel. It is also a common ingredient in soups and salads. It has a low glycemic index, and is an excellent source of iron, protein and soluble and insoluble fibre.

Garden Vegetable Casserole with Rice

Phase 2 • Makes 4 to 6 servings

2 cups	cooked brown or basmati rice
2 cups	no-fat or 1% cottage cheese
2 tbsp	parmesan cheese, grated
1	medium onion, chopped
2	medium carrots, diced
1	medium green bell pepper, diced
3 cloves	garlic, finely chopped
1 tbsp	extra virgin olive oil
1	medium zucchini, diced
1 can (19 oz/540 ml)	diced Italian tomatoes, drained
1 tbsp	dried oregano
1 tsp	salt
¼ tsp	black pepper
½ cup	low-fat mozzarella cheese, grated

Nutrition Tip

Zucchini is a dark green summer squash which resembles (in shape and size) a cucumber. The most tender and flavourful zucchini are young and no longer than 7 to 8 inches. They can be eaten raw or cooked in a variety of ways: fried, sautéed, broiled or grilled. Zucchini is a good source of folate, potassium and vitamin A.

1. Preheat over to 350°F.

2. Spread rice over the bottom of a lightly oiled 9 x 13 inch baking dish.

3. Mix the cottage cheese and parmesan cheese in bowl and spread over rice base.

4. In a large frying pan, sauté the onions, carrots, green pepper and garlic in oil until tender.

5. Add zucchini, diced tomatoes, oregano, salt and pepper to onion mixture. Reduce heat to simmer and cook covered for 5 minutes.

6. Spoon mixture over cottage cheese and top with grated mozzarella.

7. Bake 30 minutes or until bubbling.

Meatless

85

Lentil Spaghetti Sauce

Phase 1 • Makes 6 servings

1	large onion, chopped
2 stalks	celery, chopped
3 cloves	garlic, chopped
1 tbsp	olive oil
1¼ cups	dried red lentils, rinsed and drained
3 cups	water
1 can (19 oz/540 ml)	diced tomatoes with juice
2 cans (5.5 oz/156 ml)	tomato paste
2 tbsp	parsley, chopped
1 tsp	dried oregano
1 tsp	salt
¼ tsp	cayenne pepper
garnish	parmesan cheese, grated

1. Heat oil in a large pot over medium-high heat. Add onion, celery, and garlic and sauté for about 5 minutes, or until tender. Add lentils and water. Cover and cook on low for about ½ hour, or until lentils are tender. Stir often.

2. Add tomatoes, tomato paste and seasonings. Cook covered for about 15 minutes, or until lentils are soft and mushy. Add more water (up to 1 cup) if sauce becomes too thick.

3. Serve over cooked spaghetti squash (Phase 1) or spaghetti (Phase 2). Sprinkle with parmesan cheese.

Nutrition Tip

In addition to being a source of vitamin C, folate and potassium, tomatoes are also rich in a substance called "lycopene." Lycopene, found in higher quantities in cooked tomato products, is a powerful antioxidant that has been linked to a reduced incidence of cancer and heart disease.

Lentil Spaghetti Sauce

Roasted Yam Fajitas

Phase 2 • Makes 6 to 8 servings

6 or 8	whole wheat tortillas, 7- to 8-inch

FILLING

3	medium yams or sweet potatoes, peeled and cut into fries
2	carrots, julienned
1 each	medium red and green bell peppers, cut into strips
1	medium onion, sliced
2 tbsp	olive oil
to taste	salt and pepper

SAUCE

⅓ cup	orange juice
1 tsp	lime rind, grated
2 tbsp	lime juice (juice from one lime)
1 tbsp	olive oil
1 tbsp	garlic, minced
1 tsp	dried oregano
1 tsp	ground cumin
¼ tsp	hot pepper flakes

Nutrition Tip

Yam or sweet potato? Because of their similarities in size and shape, these two starchy vegetables are often thought to be related; however, they actually originate from two different species. Both have a lower glycemic index than potatoes and are packed with more beta-carotene.

1. Preheat oven to 350°F; place baking sheet in oven while preheating.

2. Filling: Toss yams, carrots, peppers and onion with oil. Place on baking sheet; sprinkle with salt and pepper to taste. Bake at 350°F for 20 to 25 minutes or until tender but not mushy.

3. Sauce: In a large bowl, combine orange juice, lime zest and juice, oil, garlic, oregano, cumin, hot pepper flakes. Add roasted vegetables and toss until coated.

4. Place vegetables in centre of tortillas and wrap.

Meatless

Sweet and Sour Tofu

Phase 1 • Makes 3 to 4 servings

1 tbsp	olive oil
1	onion, diced
2 cloves	garlic, minced
1 tbsp	fresh ginger, grated and peeled
2 or 3	carrots, sliced diagonally
1 each	green and red bell peppers, julienned
1 pkg (350 g)	extra firm tofu, drained and diced into 1 inch cubes
1 can (14 oz/398 ml)	pineapple chunks, drained (reserve juice)

SAUCE

	reserved pineapple juice
2 tbsp	brown sugar
¼ cup	vinegar
1 tbsp	cornstarch
2 tbsp	soy sauce

1. Mix sauce ingredients in a small bowl; set aside.

2. In a large frying pan over medium heat, sauté olive oil, onion, garlic and ginger for 5 minutes. Add carrots, peppers, tofu and pineapple.

3. Add sauce to frying pan. Bring to boil stirring constantly, then reduce heat and simmer for 2 to 3 minutes.

Nutrition Tip

Tofu is made from soy beans. Soy and ground flaxseed are the best dietary sources of phytoestrogens (isoflavones). Isoflavones have been shown to lower blood levels of bad cholesterol (LDL), increase good cholesterol (HDL), increase bone density and lower risk of breast cancer. 100 grams (3.5 oz) of tofu or 3 tablespoons of soy protein powder provide 75 mg of isoflavones, which is an excellent source towards your daily requirement.

Tofu Lasagna

Phase 1 • Makes 6 to 8 servings

3 tbsp	extra virgin olive oil
1	zucchini, chopped
2	red bell peppers, chopped
1	medium onion, chopped
4 cloves	garlic, coarsely chopped
1 jar (24 oz/700 ml)	Italian tomato sauce
½ tsp each	dried oregano and dried basil
1 cup	mushrooms, sliced with stems removed
1 cup	low-fat mozzarella cheese, grated
1 pkg (300 g)	soft tofu
1 pkg (300 g)	frozen spinach, drained
2 pkgs (350 g each)	extra firm tofu
½ cup	parmesan cheese, grated

1. Preheat oven to 350°F.

2. In a frying pan over medium-high heat, add 2 tablespoons of the olive oil and sauté zucchini, peppers, onion and garlic until onions are transparent.

3. In a large bowl combine tomato sauce, oregano, basil, and mushrooms.

4. In another bowl, mix soft tofu with spinach.

5. Slice extra firm tofu into ⅛-inch to ¼-inch slices to act as lasagna noodles.

6. Oil a 9 x 13 inch lasagna pan with the remaining olive oil. Pour a thin layer of tomato sauce on the bottom. Add a layer of tofu as you would lasagna noodles. Top with some of the spinach mixture and then some grilled vegetables. Sprinkle some mozzarella on top.

7. Repeat until all ingredients are used (you will have 2 or 3 layers). Top with remaining mozzarella and lastly sprinkle with parmesan cheese.

8. Bake for 45 minutes to 1 hour.

Meatless

Tofu Lasagna

Tortilla Bean Pie

Phase 2 • Makes 6 to 8 servings

2 tbsp	olive oil
1 can (12 oz/341 ml)	corn kernels, drained
½	medium onion, chopped
2 cloves	garlic, minced
1	large red bell pepper, chopped
1 can (19 oz/540 ml)	kidney beans, rinsed and drained
1 can (19 oz/540 ml)	black beans, rinsed and drained
1 cup	Tomato Salsa (page 37) or store-bought equivalent
1 tsp	chili powder
1 tsp	ground cumin
1½ cups	low-fat cheddar cheese, grated
4	flaxseed tortillas, 8 inch

1. Preheat oven to 375°F. Spray an 8-inch springform pan with cooking spray.

2. In a medium saucepan, heat 1 teaspoon of the olive oil over medium heat. Add corn and cook until browned, 6 to 7 minutes. Remove corn and set aside.

3. In remaining oil, sauté onion, garlic and red bell pepper 6 to 7 minutes. Set aside.

4. Blend beans, salsa, chili powder, and cumin in a food processor or with a hand-held blender until smooth.

5. Place one tortilla in the bottom of an 8-inch spring-form pan. Top with a third of the bean mixture, then a third of the vegetable mixture, then a quarter of the cheese mixture.

6. Repeat layering of tortilla, bean, vegetables and cheese twice more, cheese being the last ingredient on top.

7. Cover with foil and bake 40 to 45 minutes until heated through and cheese is melted.

8. Remove side of springform pan. Cut pie into wedges and serve.

Nutrition Tip

Black beans are a good source of soluble fiber and are low-glycemic, which causes a slow rise in blood sugar following a meal. Other good choices are chickpeas, navy beans, white beans, kidney beans and lentils.

Vegetarian Quiche with a Basmati Crust

Phase 2 • Makes 6 servings

CRUST

1½ cups	cooked basmati rice
2 tbsp	parmesan cheese, grated
1	egg white (reserve yolk for filling)

FILLING

5	eggs, beaten plus one yolk (remaining from crust ingredients)
1 cup	skim milk
2 tbsp	parmesan cheese, grated
1	red bell pepper, diced
1	medium zucchini, grated
¼ cup	fresh cilantro, chopped
½ cup	low-fat swiss or mozzarella cheese, grated
1 tbsp	Italian spice
½ tsp	black pepper
1	tomato, thinly sliced

Nutrition Tip
Rice, particularly sticky rice and regular white rice, tends to be higher glycemic than other grains. The lower glycemic rices include basmati (G.I. 58), parboiled (G.I. 38), long grain (G.I. 55). Choose these more often and keep serving sizes to ½ cup cooked.

1. Preheat oven to 350°F.

2. Crust: Mix together rice, parmesan cheese and egg white. Press into a 9-inch quiche pan or pie plate.

3. Filling: Mix eggs, milk, cheese, red bell pepper, zucchini, cilantro, cheese and spices and pour into crust. Layer tomato slices on top.

4. Bake 45 minutes.

5. Serve with salsa.

Meatless

Lentil Loaf

Phase 2 • Makes 6 servings

¾ cup	dried green lentils, rinsed and drained
1½ cups	vegetable stock
1	bay leaf
1 tsp	olive oil
1	medium onion, finely chopped
1 clove	garlic, minced
2 stalks	celery, finely chopped
1	red bell pepper, finely chopped
1	green bell pepper, finely chopped
1½ cups	fresh whole grain bread crumbs, loosely packed
2 tbsp	cilantro, chopped
2 tbsp	lemon juice
3	eggs
to taste	black pepper, fresh ground

1. Place lentils in a large saucepan with vegetable stock and bay leaf. Bring to boil and reduce heat to a simmer for 40 to 45 minutes or until lentils are soft and water has been absorbed.

2. Preheat oven to 350°F.

3. In a large frying pan, sauté the onion and garlic until soft. Add celery and peppers and continue to cook 3 more minutes.

4. Add lentils to vegetables, discarding bay leaf. Add bread crumbs, cilantro, lemon juice, eggs and pepper to season. Mix well.

5. Spoon mixture into loaf pan and bake 35 to 40 minutes or until firm to touch. Let sit 5 minutes before turning out.

Nutrition Tip

Lentils are a great source of fibre, B vitamins and protein, without excessive calories. They can be cooked quickly and, unlike dried beans, do not need to be soaked. Lentils come in red, brown and green. Brown and green hold their shape better and are usually used in salads and loaves. On the other hand, red lentils, which break down during cooking, are used in sauces and soups. The combination of lentils with a grain, in this case the bread crumbs, provides a complete protein.

Dave's Dal with Chickpeas

Phase 1 • Makes 4 to 6 servings
This dish is most flavourful if made ahead of time.

1 cup	dried red lentils, rinsed and drained
3 cups	vegetable stock or water
2 tbsp	canola oil
2 tsp	ground cumin
2 tsp	garlic purée (or 2 to 3 cloves put through a press)
1	onion, finely chopped
1 can (19 oz/540 ml)	chickpeas, rinsed and drained
1 tbsp	mild Indian curry paste
½ tsp	salt

Nutrition Tip
Some people avoid beans, peas and lentils because of the uncomfortable and potentially embarrassing consequences. When preparing your own beans, there are steps you can take to reduce gas (see below). Beano™ works well too.

1. In a medium pot, combine lentils with vegetable stock or water and bring to a boil. Cover, reduce heat and simmer for 15 minutes.

2. While the lentils are cooking, combine oil, cumin and garlic in a frying pan and sauté for 1 minute. Add the onion and continue to sauté for another 3 to 5 minutes, stirring constantly. Remove from heat and add to cooked lentils.

3. Add the chickpeas and stir in the curry paste and the salt.

For Phase 2, serve over rice.

PREPARING DRIED BEANS
Lentils, peas and beans are nutritious, versatile and easy to prepare. Lentils and split peas do not require soaking before cooking and are added dry to most recipes, whereas beans and whole peas need to be soaked before cooking.

For every cup of dried beans or whole peas, immerse in at least 3 cups of water. Let stand 12 hours. To reduce gas, add 1 tsp of baking soda to the soaking water.

For quick soaking, slowly bring dried beans and water to a boil and boil gently for 2 to 3 minutes. Remove from heat, add 1 tsp baking soda, and let stand from 1 to 4 hours.

To cook beans, discard soaking water and add 3 cups of fresh water for every cup of soaked beans. Simmer for 1½ to 2 hours or until tender. Using a pressure cooker will save time when cooking beans.

Meatless

Fruit Yogurt Parfait

Desserts & Snacks

Fruit Yogurt Parfait

Phase 2 • Makes 4 servings

2 cups	fresh or thawed unsweetened fruit, chopped (strawberries, raspberries, blueberries, cantaloupe, mango)
2 cups	low-fat, sugar-free yogurt, any flavour
1 cup	granola (see recipe below)

1. Evenly distribute half the granola into the bottom of four parfait dishes (⅛ cup per dish).

2. Add ½ cup of fruit to each dish, then ½ cup of yogurt per dish.

3. Garnish with remaining granola (approximately ⅛ cup per dish).

Granola with a Crunch

Phase 2 • Makes 4 cups

3 cups	slow cook oats
1 cup	mixed nuts and seeds (sunflower seeds, sesame seeds, chopped walnuts, pecans, cashew or almonds
½ cup	dried, unsweetened shredded coconut
½ tsp or to taste	cinnamon
dash	salt
½ cup or to taste	maple syrup or honey
¾ cup	raisins or chopped dried fruit (optional)

1. Preheat oven to 350°F.

2. In a bowl, combine all ingredients except raisins.

3. Spread out on a rimmed baking sheet. Bake 30 minutes or a little longer, stirring occasionally. Mixture should brown evenly. For a crunchier granola, cook a little longer, taking care that it does not burn.

4. Remove from oven and add raisins or dried fruit. Cool, stirring occasionally until granola is room temperature.

Store in a sealed, air tight container.

Desserts

Apple Custard Crumble

Phase 2 • Makes 6 servings

8 cups	apples, sliced and peeled (about 8 apples)
¼ cup	sugar
2 tbsp	all-purpose flour
1 tsp	cinnamon
2	eggs
1 cup	milk
1 tsp	vanilla
1	lemon, grated rind only

CRUMBLE TOPPING

⅔ cup	slow cook oats
½ cup	brown sugar
¼ cup	whole wheat or all-purpose flour
2 tsp	cinnamon
3 tbsp	non-hydrogenated margarine

1. Preheat oven to 350°F. Lightly spray an 8-inch square glass baking dish.

2. Layer apple slices in the dish. Press to flatten.

3. In a bowl, mix sugar, flour, and cinnamon, then whisk in eggs until frothy. Whisk in milk, lemon rind and vanilla. Pour over apples.

4. Crumble Topping: In a bowl, combine oats, brown sugar, flour and cinnamon. With fingers, mix in margarine until mixture is crumbly. Sprinkle over apple mixture.

5. Bake about 50 minutes or until apples are tender, custard is thickened and topping is golden. Serve warm or cold.

Nutrition Tip

Rolled oats are easily digestible and a good source of soluble fibre. Old-fashioned slow cooking oats or steel cut oats have the lowest G.I. rating because the grain is intact and has had minimal processing. Low G.I. means the carbohydrate is digested slowly and converted gradually to blood sugar, helping you feel full and energized longer after your meal. Choose slow cook oats more often!

Tofu Fruit Custard

Phase 1 • Makes 4 servings

1 pkg (300 g)	dessert tofu, any flavour
⅓ cup	sugar
¾ cup	unsweetened frozen fruit (mango-strawberry mix is great)
½ tsp	vanilla
½ tsp	lemon juice
pinch	salt

Nutrition Tip
Fresh fruit is not always in season. Check out the unsweetened frozen fruit available in bags at your grocery store.

1. Place all ingredients in blender or food processor and blend well.

2. Pour into serving dishes and refrigerate until firm.

This also makes a delicious sauce poured over fresh fruit.

Traditional Custard Sauce

Phase 1 • Makes 1 cup

2	egg yolks, beaten
2 tbsp	sugar
½ tsp	vanilla
pinch	salt
1 cup	skim or 1% milk

1. In a bowl, mix egg yolks, salt and sugar.

2. Heat milk in a double boiler until just warm. Gradually add egg mixture, stirring constantly. Continue stirring and cook until mixture is creamy. Do not allow the mixture to boil. Remove from heat when the custard coats a spoon.

3. Add vanilla. Spoon over fruit salad or fruit.

Especially good with bananas.

Desserts

Almost Cheesecake

Phase 1 • Makes 10 muffin cups

1 cup	5% ricotta cheese
1 cup	low-fat cottage cheese
⅓ cup	sugar
1	medium egg
¼ cup	low-fat sour cream
½ tsp	cornstarch
⅛ tsp	vanilla

1. Preheat oven to 350°F. Line ten muffin tins with paper muffin cups.

2. In a food processor or blender, combine ricotta, cottage cheese and sugar. Purée until smooth. Add egg, sour cream, cornstarch and vanilla, and blend well.

3. Divide batter among muffin cups.

4. Place muffin pan into a larger pan that contains enough hot water to come half way up the sides. Bake 30 to 35 minutes or until toothpick inserted into centre comes out clean.

5. Remove muffin pan from water bath and cool.

6. Chill before serving.

May be served with fresh fruit or puréed fruit topping.

Nutrition Tip

Hard cheeses can still be eaten if moldy portions are cut off and discarded. However, if you discover mold in a soft cheese such as ricotta, cottage or brie, throw it out! The moisture in these cheeses makes it easy for microbes to infiltrate and contaminate the entire cheese.

Almost Cheesecake

Noel's Apple Bran Muffins

Phase 2 • Makes 12 muffins

¾ cup	All-Bran™ cereal
1 cup	skim milk
⅔ cup	whole wheat flour
⅓ cup	brown sugar
2 tsp	baking powder
½ tsp	baking soda
¼ tsp	salt
1 tsp	allspice
½ tsp	cloves
1½ cups	oat bran
⅔ cup	raisins
1	large apple, peeled and cut into ¼ inch cubes
1	egg, lightly beaten
2 tsp	canola oil
½ cup	applesauce (unsweetened)

1. Preheat oven to 350°F.

2. Mix the All-Bran™ and skim milk in a bowl and let stand for a few minutes.

3. In a small bowl, combine egg, oil and applesauce.

4. In a large bowl, mix flour, sugar, baking powder, baking soda, salt and spices. Stir in the oat bran, raisins and apple.

5. Add the All-Bran™ mixture and the applesauce mixture to the dry ingredients.

6. Spoon into an oil-sprayed 12-muffin pan. Bake 20 minutes or until lightly browned.

Noel's Apple Muffins

Peanut Butter Granola Bars

Phase 2 • Makes 63 small squares
This is a high energy bar that is great after workouts and sports.

1 cup	natural peanut butter
⅓ cup	brown sugar, tightly packed
½ cup	honey
⅓ cup	non-hydrogenated margarine
2 tsp	vanilla
3 cups	slow cook oats
½ cup	coconut
½ cup	sunflower seeds
½ cup	raisins
¼ cup	ground flaxseed
½ cup	almonds, sliced
½ cup	chocolate chips

1. Preheat oven to 350°F.

2. Cream peanut butter, brown sugar, honey, margarine and vanilla together until smooth.

3. Add oats, coconut, sunflower seeds, raisins, flax meal, almonds and chocolate chips. Mix well. Pat into oiled 13 x 9 baking dish.

4. Bake 20 to 25 minutes. Cool on a rack. Cut when cool.

Including Healthy Fats in Your Diet

- Cut back on the total amount of fat you consume and emphasize healthier fats such as olive oil, canola oil and flaxseed oil.
- Choose whole grains, vegetables and fruits more often.
- Choose fish, leaner cuts of meat and lower-fat dairy products.
- Limit your intake of fat from oils, spreads, sauces, desserts and greasy snack food.
- Read labels and avoid trans fat.

Fiber Feast Bread

Phase 2 • Makes 16 slices/servings

½ cup	boiling water
1 cup	raisins
1	egg, beaten
¼ cup	brown sugar
1 cup	buttermilk
1 cup	whole wheat flour
1 cup	slow cook oats
1 cup	100% bran cereal (such as All Bran™ or Fibre 1™)
¼ cup	wheat germ
1½ tsp	baking soda
½ tsp	salt

1. Preheat oven to 350°F. Lightly oil a loaf pan with non-stick spray.

2. In a large bowl, pour boiling water over raisins and let cool. Add egg, sugar and buttermilk.

3. In another bowl, combine flour, oats, bran cereal, wheat germ, soda and salt. Mix well.

4. Stir dry ingredients into raisin mixture until well blended. Pour into loaf pan.

5. Bake 45 to 50 minutes, or until loaf tests done.

Nutrition Tip
We need more fiber. It is estimated that people need twice as much fiber as they're getting now. Your intake should be at least 25 grams of fiber per day. Oats are an excellent source of soluble fiber which helps in the regulation of blood sugar and lowering blood cholesterol levels. Other good sources of soluble fiber include: oat bran, legumes (dried beans, peas and lentils), brown rice, barley and pectin rich fruit: apples, strawberries and citrus fruits.

Snacks

Mini Pita Fruit Snack

Phase 2 • Makes 1 serving

¼	apple or pear, chopped
pinch	cinnamon
1	mini whole wheat pita
2 tsp	low-fat cheddar or mozzarella cheese, grated

1. Cut slit in pita for opening.

2. Sprinkle chopped fruit with cinnamon.

3. Spoon fruit into top of pita. Top with cheese.

Tortilla Chips

Phase 2 • Makes 64 large chips (1 serving is 4 to 6 chips)

8	8-inch flour tortillas
1 tbsp	olive oil
to taste	seasoning of choice (Italian, garlic and chili, lemon and herb)

1. Preheat oven to 375°F.

2. Lightly brush olive oil on top of each tortilla. Stack 4 tortillas, then with kitchen scissors or a long knife, cut into eight wedges.

3. Place on a cookie sheet. Sprinkle with seasonings and parmesan cheese and bake for 15 minutes. Be careful not to over brown.

Tortilla chips will keep up to 2 weeks in an airtight plastic bag at room temperature.

Roasted Almonds

Phase 1 • 1 serving is 6 to 8 almonds)
Try this simple way to flavour raw almonds. They're great as salad toppings and snacks.

1 to 2 cups	raw almonds
1	egg white, beaten
to taste	various spices and flavourings, such as chili seasoning, cajun seasoning, sugar, cinnamon, spicy Dijon mustard

1. Preheat oven to 325°F.

2. Whip egg white in bowl with whisk; add almonds. Coat well and divide into 4 portions. Add spices to taste to make a variety of flavours.

3. To keep flavours separate, make aluminum foil trays by folding up the sides to resemble shoebox lids. Add flavoured nuts.

4. Bake 2 minutes.

> **Nutrition Tip**
> Almonds are a good source of calcium and iron. A snack of dried apricots and almonds provides carbohydrates, protein, fibre and iron. For convenience, prepackage apricots and almonds in snack-size zip-lock bags. Portioning out the snack ahead of time will help prevent you from eating too much.

Chickpea Snacks

Phase 1 • 1 serving is ¼ cup

2 cans (19 oz/540 ml)	chickpeas, drained and rinsed
1 tbsp	olive oil
1 tsp	salt
½ tsp	ground cumin
½ tsp	turmeric powder
½ tsp	ground coriander
½ tsp	chili powder
½ tsp	garlic powder

1. Preheat oven to 400°F.

2. In a large bowl or a large plastic bag, toss chickpeas with oil and spices. Spread onto large baking sheets in a single layer.

3. Bake 45 minutes to 1 hour, shaking a few times during baking. Chickpeas will be golden brown when done. Remove and let cool.

Store in a paper bag to keep fresh.

Snacks

Healthy Snack Ideas

PHASE 1 SNACKS

Nutrition Tip
Keep healthy snacks handy!
It is important to keep your
blood sugar relatively level
by eating every 3 to 4 hours.
You are less likely to grab
an unhealthy snack if you
avoid becoming overly
hungry.

- 6 celery sticks with 2 tablespoons low-fat cream cheese
- 1 sliced apple with 1 tablespoon peanut butter
- 1 sliced pear with 1 tablespoon soft goat cheese (20 % MF or less)
- 1 cup fresh fruit salad with 1 tablespoon sunflower seeds
- 4 dried apricot halves with 4 walnuts (or 6 almonds)
- 1 cup vegetable juice with 6 almonds
- 1 apple with low-fat cheese string
- 1 cup grapes with 6 plain almonds
- low-fat cheese string rolled up in 1 slice of deli meat (chicken, turkey, ham, beef; buy oven-roasted meats only, as most others are full of preservatives)
- ½ cup cottage cheese, ½ sliced banana, 1 teaspoon vanilla and sweetener of choice (optional)
- 1 cup heated skim milk, 1 teaspoon vanilla
- ½ cup Jello™ sugar-free pudding with ¼ cup slivered almonds
- ½ cup raw vegetables with 2 tablespoons Hummus (see recipe page 39)

PHASE 2 SNACKS

- all phase 1 snacks
- 1 hard boiled egg with a Wasa™ cracker
- 2 low-glycemic crackers (i.e. Wasa™, Ryvita™) with 1 tablespoon peanut butter
- oven-roasted deli meats with 1 Wasa™ cracker and a pickle
- 6 to 8 homemade pita chips with salsa (see recipe page 102)

CARDIOVASCULAR DISEASE IN YOUTH

Studies are now showing us that children ages 10 to 18 have evidence of early "hardening of the arteries" or cardiovascular disease. This has been documented via ultrasound of their arteries. Childhood obesity is also at epidemic proportions, primarily due to the insulin resistance they are developing so early in life because of poor food choices and lack of exercise. This can be reversed through low-glycemic eating, more emphasis on fruits and vegetables, and 60 to 90 minutes of activity throughout the day.

Menu Planning

The following menu plan demonstrates how to incorporate recipes into a program such as Dr. Strand's *Healthy for Life*. Please note that if you have started your dietary changes with a five-day low-glycemic fibre cleanse, feel free to include extra vegetables, vegetable salads or a home made vegetable soup, such as Clean Sweep Soup on page 35, if you miss chewing or are hungry.

PHASE 1

As mentioned on page 11, Phase 1 eliminates breads, grains, rice, cereal, pasta, potatoes, sugar, candy, donuts, juices, and pop. This will help diminish carbohydrate cravings and reverse insulin resistance. All Phase 1 recipes on the following menu plans are interchangeable.

PHASE 2

This maintenance phase re-introduces some breads, rice, cereals, and potatoes that will not spike your blood sugar. These include carbohydrates with a lower glycemic index. Sugary treats, pop and junk food should be a rarity in any diet. Phase 2 allows you the freedom of substituting any recipe, Phase 1 or 2, for another.

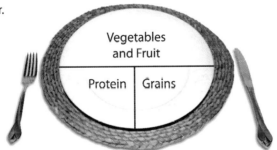

How to portion your plate

TIPS FOR CONTINUED SUCCESS

- Eat at regular times.
- Choose a variety of foods from all food groups.
- Avoid or limit sugars and sweets.
- Reduce the amount of saturated and trans fats that you eat. Include more healthy fats (olive, canola and flaxseed oils).
- Include high fibre foods.
- Limit salt, alcohol and caffeine.
- Try something new! Low-glycemic choices such as barley, bulgur, lentils, or quinoa can help prevent boredom.
- When choosing a nutritional bar, look for one with a low glycemic rating.

Weight Loss Phase 1: One Week Sample Menu

For optimal nutrition, this meal plan should be complemented with a high quality nutritional supplement including calcium and vitamin D. To keep hydrated, drink 6 to 8 glasses of water daily.

	Monday	Tuesday	Wednesday	Thursday	Friday	Saturday	Sunday
BREAKFAST	Nutrition Shake	Nutrition Shake	Nutrition Shake	Nutrition Shake	• Omelette with Salsa *page 37* • ½ cup fresh fruit	Nutrition Shake	Nutrition Shake
SNACK	Nutritional Bar	• 1 cup assorted raw vegetables • 2 tbsp Tzatziki or 2 tbsp Hummus *pages 38-39*	Nutritional Bar	Nutritional Bar	¾ cup Chickpea Snacks *page 103*	• Nutritional Bar • 1 glass skim or soy milk	• ¾ cup low-fat sugar-free yogurt • ¼ cup raw almonds
LUNCH	Nutrition Shake	Tuna Citrus Spinach Salad *page 33*	Nutrition Shake	Nutrition Shake	Nutrition Shake	• Lettuce Wraps *page 29* • 1 glass skim or soy milk	Nutrition Shake
SNACK	• ¾ cup low-fat sugar-free yogurt • ½ cup fresh fruit	• Nutritional Bar • 1 glass skim or soy milk	Fruit Yogurt Parfait *page 95*	• ¾ cup low-fat cottage cheese • 1 cup assorted raw vegetables	Nutritional Bar	• 1 cup assorted raw vegetables • 2 tbsp Hummus *page 39*	• Nutritional Bar • 1 glass skim or soy milk
DINNER	• Spicy Pineapple Chicken *page 23* • side salad with 2 tbsp low-fat dressing	Nutrition Shake	• Dijon Chicken *page 24* • Basic Coleslaw *page 57*	• Sweet and Sour Tofu *page 88* • 1 cup assorted raw vegetables • Fast Veggie Dip *page 38*	Nutrition Shake	Nutrition Shake	• West Coast Teriyaki Salmon *page 74* • side salad with 2 tbsp low-fat dressing • ½ cup fresh fruit

Maintenance Phase 2: One Week Sample Menu

For optimal nutrition, this meal plan should be complemented with a high quality nutritional supplement including calcium and vitamin D.
To keep hydrated, drink 6 to 8 glasses of water daily.

	Monday	Tuesday	Wednesday	Thursday	Friday	Saturday	Sunday
BREAKFAST	Nutrition Shake	Nutrition Shake	• On-the-Run Breakfast *page 20* • 1 glass skim or soy milk	• Egg Tortilla Bowls *page 45* • ½ cup fresh fruit	• Egg in a Nest *page 20* • ½ grapefruit	Nutrition Shake	Nutrition Shake
SNACK	Nutritional Bar	• 1 to 2 cups assorted raw vegetables • 2 tbsp Tzatziki *page 38*	• ½ cup low-fat cottage cheese with ½ tsp vanilla (optional) and sweetener to taste • 1 cup assorted raw vegetables	Nutritional Bar	• ¾ cup low-fat sugar-free yogurt • ½ cup fresh fruit	Nutritional Bar	Nutritional Bar
LUNCH	• Quick Chicken Soup *page 23* • celery and carrot sticks	• Quick Beef Chili *page 28* • 1 slice flax bread	Nutrition Shake	• Mix & Match Wrap *page 34* • 1 cup assorted raw vegetables • 2 tbsp low-fat dressing • 1 glass skim or soy milk	Nutrition Shake	• Amazing Quiche *page 46* • Broccoli Walnut Salad *page 58* • 2 tbsp low-fat dressing	• Creamy Roasted Vegetable Soup *page 54* • 1 slice whole wheat bread • ½ cup grapes
SNACK	• ¼ cup raw almonds • 1 whole fruit (ie. kiwi) • 1 glass skim or soy milk	Nutritional Bar	Nutritional Bar	• 1 cup Basic Salad *page 55* • 2 tbsp Yogurt Dill Dressing *page 55* • ½ tin water packed salmon	Nutritional Bar	• 1 slice Fibre Feast Bread *page 101* • 1 glass skim or soy milk	• Apple Bran Muffin *page 99* • ¼ cup raw almonds • 1 glass skim or soy milk
DINNER	• Italian Tuna Sauce *page 32* • ½ cup whole wheat pasta • side salad with 2 tbsp low-fat dressing	• Thai Chicken Tortilla Pizza *page 24* • side salad with 2 tbsp low-fat dressing	• Jiffy Ground Beef Stir-fry *page 28* • ½ cup basmati rice	• Nutrition Shake • 1 to 2 cups Basic Salad *page 55* • 2 tbsp low-fat dressing (optional)	• Roasted Yam Fajitas *page 87* • 1 to 2 cups Basic Salad *page 55* • 2 tbsp low-fat dressing	• Tofu Lasagna *page 89* • side salad with 2 tbsp low-fat dressing • 1 glass red wine (optional)	• Halibut in White Wine *page 76* • Colourful Black Bean & Corn Salad *page 59* • ½ cup fresh fruit

ARE YOU EATING BECAUSE OF HUNGER?

Sometimes we use food to satisfy feelings other than hunger. The next time you are thinking about eating, take a moment to figure out if you are truly hungry. You might instead be experiencing emotions that are triggering your desire to eat. Say "HALT" out loud before you reach for a snack. HALT stands for "Hungry, Angry, Lonely or Tired. Which are you feeling? If it's not hunger, food is not the solution.

COMMON QUESTIONS

What should I do if carbohydrate cravings return?

Inevitably, you will at some time eat too many high-glycemic carbohydrates over a short period of time. This could happen on a vacation, during the holidays, or it may simply be the result of slipping into unhealthy eating patterns. It is important to recognize this situation quickly and get back on track. Otherwise, you will once again begin to get hungry and crave high-glycemic carbohydrates. When this happens it is wise to figure out what got you back into this pattern.

The best way to reduce this carbohydrate addiction is to return to Phase 1 of the *Heathy for Life* program. In Phase 1 you need to avoid all sugar, bread, flour, cereals, rice, pasta, and potatoes. The medical literature shows us that this is a critical time in any healthy lifestyle program, and failure to recognize these signs early can lead to a major setback. Once you have gained control of your cravings and your appetite is reduced, you can slowly return to Phase 2.

How do I order low-glycemic foods when eating in restaurants?

When eating out, plan in advance. Try to choose a restaurant that has a menu offering healthy choices such as grilled fish, meat and poultry dishes, and lots of fresh vegetables and salads. Keep in mind that portion sizes are usually larger than those at home. You need to be assertive and ask for your meal the way you want it. Here are some tips:

- Order a green salad with lots of vegetables to start with a low-fat dressing on the side so you can control the amount you use. Salads have a very low G.I. rating and will help you fill up before the main course arrives.

- Order an entrée with more emphasis on protein and vegetables. For example, a chicken and veggie stir-fry or a dinner size salad topped with grilled chicken, beef or fish are excellent choices.

- Avoid bread and starchy side dishes. Ask for a side salad instead of mashed potatoes, fries or rice.

- Instead of ordering one large entrée, order two appetizers, or an appetizer and a salad, as your meal.

- Consider sharing an entrée with a friend.

- Eat slowly. The stomach can take up to 30 minutes to let your brain know you are full.

- Ask that the rice or potatoes be held and that the vegetables be doubled.

The Importance of Cellular Nutrition

For years, it was believed that people could get all the nutrients they needed from their diet. However, after researching the medical literature and working with physicians such as Dr. Ray Strand, it became apparent that every man, woman, and child needs to be taking nutritional supplements in order to better protect their health and minimize oxidative stress.

What is oxidative stress?

As the body utilizes the oxygen needed to sustain life, occasionally a charged oxygen molecule is produced called a free radical. If the free radical is not neutralized by an antioxidant, it can go on to create even more volatile free radicals. These highly reactive free radicals damage cell walls and vessels, proteins, fats and even the DNA nucleus of a cell.

Free radical damage is caused by:

- excessive emotional stress
- radiation from the sun
- cigarette smoke
- excessive exercise
- poor diet – high-glycemic and high-fat
- pollutants in our air, food and water
- medication
- elevated blood sugar (caused by type 1 or type 2 diabetes)

How can you minimize oxidative damage?

The best way is to ensure you have enough antioxidants available to handle the number of free radicals produced. If not, oxidative stress occurs and the body is vulnerable to degeneration similar to rust on a car. The body produces some antioxidants and we are able to get additional antioxidants from our food — primarily from fruits and vegetables.

Unfortunately, there is a a gap in our protection because our foods have become significantly depleted of antioxidants and supporting minerals as a result of mineral depletion in the soil, green harvesting and loss of nutrients through over processing and long transportation distances. The gap is widened further by our poor food choices and food preparation methods. Research has shown that the general population consumes significantly less than the recommended intake for calcium, vitamin D, chromium, selenium, copper, folic acid, vitamins B6 and B12, and vitamin E. Similarly, studies show that well over 50 percent of children do not get the daily recommended intakes (DRI) of many nutrients.

Oxidative stress has now been shown via medical research to be the root cause of over 70 chronic degenerative diseases, including heart disease, stroke, cancer, type 2 diabetes, arthritis, Alzheimer's dementia, macular degeneration, lupus, MS, and the list goes on.

What is the answer to oxidative stress and poor quality diets?

Nutritional supplements are the answer because it is difficult to get all the nutrients you need from your diet — even with healthy eating. Consider what you must eat to receive an optimal amount of 400 IU of vitamin E, one of the most powerful antioxidants to combat free radicals: 33 pounds of spinach, 5.2 pounds of wheat germ, 2.2 pounds of almonds, or 1 quart of safflower oil!

CRITERIA FOR CHOOSING A GOOD QUALITY NUTRITIONAL SUPPLEMENT

Is it a pharmaceutical grade nutritional supplement?

The nutritional supplement industry is basically an unregulated industry. There is no guarantee that what is on the label is actually in the tablet. You need to select a company that manufactures their products according to pharmaceutical grade Good Manufacturing Practices (GMP). This means that they purchase pharmaceutical grade raw ingredients and then produce them with the same quality control as they would medications. You will be guaranteed that you are getting what you paid for.

Does it meet US Pharmacopoeia (USP)?

When the company follows USP guidelines, it gives you the assurance that your tablets will dissolve. Unfortunately, many supplements fall short and do not meet the USP.

Is your supplement complete and balanced?

According to Dr. Strand, supplements need to provide optimal levels of several different antioxidants and their supporting B co-factors (vitamins B1, B2, B5, B6, B12 and folic acid) along with the minerals selenium, magnesium, zinc, copper, manganese, chromium and vanadium. Your body needs these nutrients in the proper balance to create a synergy. Synergy means that the nutrients work together at the cellular level to enhance the body's natural immune system.

For more information on choosing a good quality supplement and which ones have the best ratings, check out Lyle MacWilliam's book *Nutrisearch Comparative Guide to Nutrition Supplements 4th edition*, which rates over 1400 U.S. and Canadian supplements. It is available at www.comparativeguide.com.

Move It and Lose It!

WHY WORKING OUT WORKS!

You now have the tools to prepare healthy fast meals, but this is only one component to improving your health. Today's society has been more educated in the need to incorporate fitness into their lifestyle than previous generations, yet we are becoming heavier at an alarming rate! We have become inactive, lazy and unhealthy to the point that we are increasing our risk of diabetes, hypertension, cardiovascular disease and many cancers. That's only part of the picture. When inactive, our bodies begin to experience aching muscles and joints, back problems, fatigue and even psychological effects such as depression. As our fitness levels drop, so does our self- esteem.

But there is great news too! Once we begin to implement a good fitness program, we experience a multitude of health improvements, including weight management, elevated moods, better sleep patterns, fewer health problems, and an improved immune system. Those who have embraced both optimal nutrition and an exercise program also notice they have better concentration (especially important for children and school work) and the more "mature" generation, including the baby boomers, look and feel years younger! It is never to late to get started. Only you can make the decision to change your life and health for the better. That decision could enable you to live a long, healthy life that is filled with active living well beyond retirement. We must face the fact that we are literally growing old before our time. The key to slowing the aging process is exercise. When you nurture and support your body with regular exercise and healthy nutrition, your body reciprocates with more energy plus weight control. Taking care of your body, no matter what your age, is an investment. The return is priceless.

Create a Positive Mindset for Exercise

Our bodies require a complete fitness program that includes aerobic exercise, muscular strength, endurance conditioning, and flexibility exercise. The key to maintaining any fitness program is mental attitude. We all know that exercise can be monotonous, boring, strenuous and tiring. However, the reality is, if you want to slow the aging process and invest in your body for a better quality of life, exercise needs to be as important to you as brushing your teeth every day. When you change your mind set and look at exercise from a totally different point of view, like a 'need to have' instead of a 'nice to have', it is amazing how much easier it is to find time for some form of exercise each day. This positive mindset is one of the key components to slowing the aging process and enabling us to have life-long weight control.

Exercise Leads to Health

Weight bearing exercise will build stronger muscles, joints and bones. Muscular conditioning can improve strength and posture, and reduce the risk of lower back injury; it is also an important component of a weight management program. Aerobic exercise does wonders for your cardiovascular system and improves the immune systems, cholesterol levels, blood pressure and stress levels. Flexibility exercise is needed to maintain joint range of motion and reduce the risk of injury and muscle soreness.

GETTING STARTED

If you haven't been active for some time, start with small obtainable goals. Use a calendar to book an appointment with yourself three time per week. For some it may mean a walk around the block, gradually adding an additional block as fitness levels improve. Don't set yourself up for failure by overwhelming yourself with unrealistic goals. Begin with one-week, one-month and three-month goals.

For those who have been active, congratulations, keep up the good work! If you find yourself losing interest due to boredom, try a new sport or activity, join a fitness facility, or find a fitness partner to keep each other accountable. When you hit a plateau, it's time to shake things up. Interval training is a great way to push yourself to new fitness levels. For those who have access to a treadmill, walking at a moderate pace and using different incline settings can really be effective. A 30-minute workout that includes one-minute high-intensity "pushes" three to five times during the half hour can really improve the cardiovascular system.

Strength Training

You may consider calisthenics, free weights or machines. Just be sure that your strength training includes exercises for every major muscle group, including the muscles of the arms, chest, back, stomach, hips and legs. Beginners may choose to start training two times a week, while the more experienced may train three to five times a week. Consider hiring a certified trainer to put you on a program appropriate to your fitness level. Learning proper form can prevent possible injuries and setbacks. Weight bearing exercise can help in building and sustaining bone density.

Aerobic Exercise

Three to four days of aerobic activity will provide some health benefits. If you are trying to lose weight, aim for four or more days per week, making sure you take at least one day off a week. Work up to 30 or more minutes per session for general health maintenance. For weight loss, gradually work up to 45 minutes or longer at low to moderate intensities in a low- or no-impact activity.

You may chose a weight-bearing aerobic exercise such as walking, jogging, skipping rope, or dance exercise. Aerobic exercise is any activity that uses large muscle groups in a continuous, rhythmic fashion for sustained periods of time. There are also non-weight-bearing aerobic exercises, such as swimming, rowing, bicycling and stationary cycling.

Flexibility Exercises

These involve holding a mild stretch for 10 to 30 seconds while you breathe normally. Always warm up before you stretch. Like strength conditioning, flexibility exercises should include stretches for all the major muscle groups.

Exercise Essentials

Essentials include good shoes, comfortable workout clothing, water bottle, adequate time frame and a good attitude. Have a PLAN.

Set Yourself Some S.M.A.R.T. Goals

S = Specific   **M** = Measurable   **A** = Attainable   **R** = Realistic   **T** = within a Time frame

Remember, just like brushing our teeth each day, we need to do some form of exercise to keep healthy, alert and feeling young. However, it is important to be realistic about our goals and remember that we have the rest of our lives to be active and slow the aging process.

SIMPLE STRATEGIES FOR "EXTRA STEPS"

- Park farther away from your destination.
- Take the stairs, not the elevator or escalator.
- Get off the bus a few blocks early.
- Exercise during commercial breaks.
- Walk during your breaks and lunch hour.
- Find a walking partner for the evening.
- Walk the golf course…don't ride!
- Walk the arena or field while your child is playing their sport.
- Play games with your children that include walking and running.
- Walk your dog, or even your neighbour's dog!

Always check with your doctor before beginning any exercise program, especially if you are over 40 or have cardiovascular risk factors, such as smoking, high blood pressure, high cholesterol, diabetes or a family history of heart disease.

KEEP HYDRATED: DRINK 6 TO 8 GLASSES OF WATER DAILY

Water is our life force. We can only go a few days without water before our body begins to deteriorate and die. Our body uses water every day for all its internal cellular functions. It has been recommended that we have eight glasses of water every day to replenish what we have lost. Unfortunately, most people fall short on that prescription and may suffer from common complaints such as lack of energy, headaches, and sometimes even joint and muscle aches. When exercising, we need even more water to replace what is lost during a workout. When we are exercising the body generates heat that it must remove. When we sweat, we can effectively cool down. Heavy or prolonged sweating can lead to dehydration. This is the major cause of fatigue and poor performance. You might lose around one litre (4 full glasses) of water in an hour workout so you will need to replace it before, during and after exercising or playing sports.

Shopping List

FRESH FOODS

MEAT/POULTRY
- [ ] Chicken breast
- [ ] Turkey breast
- [ ] Ground chicken
- [ ] Ground turkey
- [ ] Lean ground beef
- [ ] Lean cuts of beef
- [ ] Wild game
- [ ] Buffalo
- [ ] Pork loin
- [ ] Turkey bacon
- [ ] Canadian (back) bacon

FISH and SEAFOOD
- [ ] Salmon
- [ ] Tuna
- [ ] Trout
- [ ] Halibut
- [ ] Sole
- [ ] Shrimp

DAIRY, EGGS and SOY
- [ ] Skim or 1% milk
- [ ] Soy milk
- [ ] Tofu
- [ ] Eggs
- [ ] Low-fat sour cream
- [ ] Low-fat plain yogurt
- [ ] Low-fat cottage cheese
- [ ] Low-fat cheeses
- [ ] Feta cheese
- [ ] Parmesan cheese

VEGETABLES
- [ ] Leafy vegetables
- [ ] Artichokes
- [ ] Asparagus
- [ ] Broccoli
- [ ] Brussels sprouts
- [ ] Cabbage
- [ ] Carrots
- [ ] Cauliflower
- [ ] Celery
- [ ] Cucumber
- [ ] Peas
- [ ] Green pepper
- [ ] Red and orange bell peppers
- [ ] Snow peas
- [ ] Spinach
- [ ] Tomato
- [ ] Zucchini
- [ ] Yams
- [ ] Green onion
- [ ] Onions
- [ ] Small new potatoes
- [ ] Mushrooms
- [ ] Frozen vegetables

FRESH HERBS
- [ ] Cilantro
- [ ] Parsley
- [ ] Mint
- [ ] Ginger
- [ ] Garlic

FRUITS
- [ ] Apples
- [ ] Blueberries
- [ ] Blackberries
- [ ] Strawberries
- [ ] Huckleberries
- [ ] Oranges
- [ ] Grapefruit
- [ ] Cherries
- [ ] Apricots
- [ ] Pears
- [ ] Peaches
- [ ] Grapes
- [ ] Pineapple
- [ ] Plums
- [ ] Kiwi fruit
- [ ] Bananas
- [ ] Lemons
- [ ] Limes
- [ ] Cranberries
- [ ] Mandarin oranges
- [ ] Mango
- [ ] Papaya
- [ ] Watermelon
- [ ] Cantaloupe
- [ ] Honeydew

Extras

_____

_____

_____

_____

_____

_____

_____

PANTRY

GRAINS
- [ ] Black beans
- [ ] Chickpeas
- [ ] Kidney beans
- [ ] Pinto beans
- [ ] Soy beans
- [ ] Lentils
- [ ] Split peas
- [ ] Slow-cook oatmeal
- [ ] Cornmeal
- [ ] Whole wheat flour
- [ ] Bran
- [ ] Barley
- [ ] Buckwheat
- [ ] Bulgur
- [ ] Quinoa
- [ ] Basmati rice
- [ ] Brown rice
- [ ] Long grain rice, parboiled
- [ ] Wild rice
- [ ] Whole wheat kernels
- [ ] Whole rye kernels
- [ ] Sprouted wheat high fibre bread
- [ ] Whole wheat wraps
- [ ] Whole wheat and vegetable pasta

CEREAL
- [ ] High fibre cereal
- [ ] All Bran™
- [ ] Bran Buds™

STAPLES
- [ ] Soy or whey protein powder
- [ ] Meal replacement powder

CANNED GOODS
- [ ] Tuna/salmon
- [ ] Beets
- [ ] Corn
- [ ] Green/yellow beans
- [ ] Tomatoes
- [ ] Tomato paste
- [ ] Mushrooms
- [ ] Mandarin oranges
- [ ] Pineapple chunks
- [ ] Pumpkin

SPICES
- [ ] Salt
- [ ] Pepper
- [ ] Allspice
- [ ] Basil
- [ ] Celery Seed
- [ ] Chili powder
- [ ] Cinnamon
- [ ] Cloves
- [ ] Cumin
- [ ] Garlic powder
- [ ] Ground ginger
- [ ] Greek seasoning
- [ ] Italian spice
- [ ] Nutmeg
- [ ] Oregano
- [ ] Thyme
- [ ] Turmeric
- [ ] Dry mustard
- [ ] Hot pepper flakes
- [ ] Curry powder
- [ ] Curry paste
- [ ] Wasabi powder
- [ ] Chicken bouillon cubes
- [ ] Beef bouillon cubes

CONDIMENTS
- [ ] Low-fat mayonnaise
- [ ] Dijon mustard
- [ ] Lemon juice
- [ ] Balsamic vinegar
- [ ] Wine vinegar
- [ ] Hot sauce
- [ ] Worcestershire sauce
- [ ] Soy sauce
- [ ] Hoisin sauce
- [ ] Teriyaki sauce

NUTS and FATS
- [ ] Natural peanut butter
- [ ] Almonds
- [ ] Sesame seeds
- [ ] Walnuts
- [ ] Flaxseed (ground)
- [ ] Flaxseed oil
- [ ] Extra virgin olive oil
- [ ] Canola oil
- [ ] Cooking spray

EXTRAS
- [ ] Raisins
- [ ] Dried cranberries
- [ ] Vanilla extract
- [ ] Almond extract
- [ ] Unflavoured gelatin
- [ ] Stevia
- [ ] Olives

Index

Appetizers:
  Dip with a Twist, 38
  Fast Veggie Dip, 38
  Hummus, 39
  Tortilla Chips, 102
  Tzatziki, 38
Apples:
  Apple Custard Crumble, 96
  Curried Chicken and Apple Salad, 63
  Homemade Muesli, 21
  Noel's Apple Bran Muffins, 99
  Salmon Waldorf Salad, 32
Artificial Sweetener:
  about, 62
Asian:
  Asian Salad, 24
  Lettuce Wraps, 29
  Szechwan Orange Ginger Chicken, 73
  Thai Peanut Sauce, 38
Bananas:
  Bananarama Tofu Boost, 19
  Chocolate, Banana Malt, 18
  Jake's Shake, 18
  Orange Creamsicle Shake, 17
  Peanut Butter Cup Smoothie, 18
  Strawberry Banana Smoothie, 17
Barley:
  about, 82
  Barley Mushroom Pilaf, 82
Beans:
  about cooking, 93
  Anya's Chickpea Burgers, 84
  Bean Burritos, 44
  Black Bean Salsa, 37
  Black Bean Soup, 49
  Chickpea Snacks, 103
  Colene's Spicy Carrot and Chickpea
  Salad, 69
  Colourful Black Bean and Corn Salad, 59
  Dave's Dal with Chickpeas, 93
  Hamburger Soup, 30
  Kidney Bean Curry (Raj Mah Di Dal), 79
  Kidney Bean, Cabbage and Feta
  Salad, 65
  Minestrone Soup, 48
  Mixed Bean Salad, 67
  Quick Chili, 28
  Quinoa and Black Bean Salad, 70
  Tabouli, 68
  Tortilla Bean Pie, 90

Beef:
  "Old Fashioned" Hearty Beef Stew, 75
  Beef and Broccoli Stir-fry, 77
  Ground Beef Stroganoff, 27
  Hamburger Soup, 30
  Jiffy Ground Beef Stir Fry, 28
  Lettuce Wraps, 29
  Mediterranean Pita Pizza, 27
  Preparing, 13
  Quick Chili, 28
  Taco Salad in a Tortilla Bowl, 29
  wrap/pita combos, 34
Beets:
  Tangy Beet Salad Ring, 64
Berries (also see specific berries):
  Lemon Tart Smoothie, 19
  Low-glycemic Shake, 17
  Old Fashioned Oatmeal, 21
  Strawberry Banana Smoothie, 17
  Sunrise High Energy Smoothie, 19
Bran:
  Fiber Feast Bread, 101
  Noel's Apple Bran Muffins, 99
  On-the-run Breakfast, 20
Breads:
  Egg in a Nest, 20
  Fiber Feast Bread, 101
  French Toast, 21
  Noel's Apple Bran Muffins, 99
  Quick Croutons, 60
Breakfast:
  Country Garden Omelet, 20
  Egg and Tofu Scramble, 43
  Egg in a Nest, 20
  Flaxseed Pancakes, 41
  French Toast, 21
  Hearty Oatmeal Pancakes, 42
  Homemade Muesli, 21
  Old Fashioned Oatmeal, 21
  On-the-run Breakfast, 20
Broccoli:
  Beef and Broccoli Stir-fry, 77
  Broccoli Walnut Salad, 58
  Jiffy Ground Beef Stir-fry, 28
Brunch:
  Egg and Tofu Scramble, 43
  Flaxseed Pancakes, 41
  Hearty Oatmeal Pancakes, 42
Bulgur Wheat:
  Greek Style Bulgur Salad, 71
  Tabouli, 68
Burgers:
  Anya's Chickpea Burgers, 84
  Tuna Burger, 31

Cabbage:
  Asian Salad, 24
  Basic Coleslaw, 57
  Big Batch Creamy Coleslaw, 62
  Kidney Bean, Cabbage and Feta
  Salad, 65
Calcium:
  about, 46, 77
Carrots:
  Asian Salad, 24
  Colene's Spicy Carrot and Chickpea
  Salad, 69
  Garden Vegetable Casserole with
  Rice, 85
  Lettuce Wraps, 29
  Orange Carrot Soup, 53
  Roasted Vegetables, 81
Cauliflower:
  Curried Sweet Potato and Cauliflower
  Soup, 52
Celery:
  Quick Chicken Soup, 23
  Salmon Waldorf Salad, 32
  Taco Salad in a Tortilla Bowl, 29
  Tuna Salad Mix, 31
Cereal:
  Homemade Muesli, 21
  Old Fashioned Oatmeal, 21
Cheese, Cheddar:
  about, 98
  Amazing Quiche, 46
  Tortilla Bean Pie, 90
Cheese, Cottage:
  about, 98
  Almost Cheesecake, 98
  Chicken Caesar Salad, 60
  Garden Vegetable Casserole with
  Rice, 85
  On-the-run Breakfast, 20
  Tropical Cheesecake Smoothie, 19
Cheese, Feta
  Greek Style Bulgur Salad, 71
  Kidney Bean, Cabbage and Feta
  Salad, 65
  Mediterranean Pita Pizza, 27
  Turkey Pesto Quesadilla, 25
Cheese, Mozzarella:
  about, 98
  Curried Tuna Pizza, 31
  Thai Chicken Tortilla Pizza, 24
  Turkey Pesto Quesadilla, 25
  Vegetarian Quiche with a Basmati
  Crust, 91

Chicken:
  Asian Salad, 24
  Chicken Caesar Salad, 60
  Curried Chicken and Apple Salad, 63
  Dijon Chicken, 24
  Fast Fusion Chicken, 26
  Indonesian Curried Salad, 25
  preparing, 13
  Quick Chicken Soup, 23
  Spicy Pineapple Chicken, 23
  Szechwan Orange Ginger Chicken, 73
  Thai Chicken Tortilla Pizza, 24
  wrap/pita combos, 34
Corn:
  Colourful Black Bean and Corn Salad, 59
Cranberries, dried:
  Cranberry Vinaigrette, 56
  Old Fashioned Oatmeal, 21
Cucumber:
  Asian Salad, 24
  Indonesian Curried Chicken Salad, 25
  Lettuce Wraps, 29
  Tzatziki, 38
Curry:
  Curried Chicken Apple Salad, 63
  Curried Sweet Potato Cauliflower
    Soup, 52
  Curried Tuna Pizza, 31
  Curry Dressing, 25
  Fast Fusion Chicken, 26
  Indonesian Curried Chicken Salad, 25
  Kidney Bean Curry (Raj Mah Di Dal), 79
Desserts:
  Almost Cheesecake, 98
  Apple Custard Crumble, 96
  Fruit Dip, 38
  Fruit Yogurt Parfait, 95
  Granola with a Crunch, 95
  Mint Yogurt Dip, 38
  Noel's Apple Bran Muffins, 99
  Peanut Butter Granola Bars, 100
  Tofu Fruit Custard, 97
  Traditional Custard Sauce, 97
Dips:
  Dip with a Twist, 38
  Fast Veggie Dip, 38
  Fruit Dip, 38
  Hummus, 39
  Mint Yogurt Dip, 38
  Tzatziki, 38

Dressings:
  Clean Sweep Salad Dressing, 36
  Cranberry Vinaigrette, 56
  Curry Dressing, 25
  Ginger Sesame Dressing, 56
  Lemon Basil Vinaigrette, 66
  Orange Vinaigrette, 55
  Salmon Waldorf Salad Dressing, 32
  Tabouli Dressing, 68
  Tuna Citrus Spinach Salad Dressing, 33
  Yogurt Dill Dressing, 55
Eggs:
  about, 21
  Amazing Quiche, 46
  Country Garden Omelette, 20
  Egg and Tofu Scramble, 43
  Egg in a Nest, 20
  Egg Tortilla Bowls, 45
  French Toast, 21
  Traditional Custard Sauce, 97
  Vegetarian Quiche with a Basmati
    Crust, 91
  wrap/pita combos, 34
Exercise:
  about, 111-113
Fats:
  about, 100
  olive oil, 61
  omega 3, 32, 58
Fiber:
  about, 79, 101
  Fiber Feast Bread, 101
Fish:
  about 13, 31, 32
  Curried Tuna Pizza, 31
  Fish Fillets on Spinach, 78
  Halibut in White Wine, 76
  Italian Tuna Sauce, 32
  Salmon Loaf, 33
  Salmon Salad, Fajitas, 32
  Salmon Waldorf Salad, 32
  Tuna Burger, 31
  Tuna Citrus Spinach Salad, 33
  Tuna Salad Mix, 31
  West Coast Teriyaki Salmon with
    Wasabi Mayonnaise, 74
  wrap/pita combos, 34
Flaxseed:
  about, 41
  Flaxseed Pancakes, 41
  Low-glycemic Shake, 17
  Peanut Butter Cup Smoothie, 18
  Sunrise High Energy Smoothie, 19

Fridge and Freezer Prep:
  about, 15
Fruit, Mixed Assorted (also see specific
    fruit):
  about, 97
  Fruit Yogurt Parfait, 95
  Homemade Muesli, 21
  Mini Pita Fruit Snack, 102
  Tofu Fruit Custard, 97
Garlic:
  about, 38
Glycemic Index:
  about, 3, 9
  tables, 10
  tips, 17
Ground Meat:
  about, 47
  Ground Beef Stroganoff, 27
  Hamburger Soup, 30
  Homemade Turkey Sausage Patties, 47
  Jiffy Ground Beef Stir-fry, 28
  Lettuce Wraps, 29
  Mediterranean Pita Pizza, 27
  preparing, 13
  Quick Chili, 28
  Taco Salad in a Tortilla Bowl, 29
  Tomato Spaghetti Sauce, 30
  wrap/pita combos, 34
Iron:
  about, 75
Juices:
  Lemon Tart Smoothie, 19
  Orange Carrot Soup, 53
  Orange Vinaigrette. 55
  Sunrise High Energy Smoothie, 19
  Szechwan Orange Ginger Chicken, 73
  Tropical Cheesecake Smoothie, 19
Lemon:
  Lemon Tart Smoothie, 19
  Quinoa and Black Bean Salad, 70
  Tabouli Dressing, 68
  Tuna Citrus Spinach Salad, 33
Lentils:
  about, 51, 92
  Dave's Dal with Chickpeas, 93
  Lentil Loaf, 92
  Lentil Rice Salad, 66
  Lentil Spaghetti Sauce, 86
  Red Lentil Soup, 50
Lettuce:
  Lettuce Wraps, 29

Main Meals:
  Beef and Broccoli Stir-fry, 77:
  Fish Fillets on Spinach, 78
  Halibut in White Wine, 76
  "Old Fashioned" Hearty Beef Stew, 75
  Szechwan Orange Ginger Chicken, 73
  West Coast Teriyaki Salmon with
    Wasabi Mayonnaise, 74
Marinades:
  Beef Stir-fry, marinade, 77
  Teriyaki, marinade, 74
Mayonnaise:
  Big Batch Creamy Coleslaw, 62
  Curried Chicken and Apple Salad, 63
  Fast Veggie Dip, 38
  Indonesian Curried Salad, 25
  Light Tartar Sauce, 39
  Salmon Waldorf Salad, 32
  Tzatziki Sauce, 38
  Wasabi Mayonnaise, 74
Meatless Meals and Side Dishes:
  Anya's Chickpea Burgers, 84
  Barley Mushroom Pilaf, 82
  Garden Vegetable Casserole with
    Rice, 85
  Kidney Bean Curry (Raj Mah Di Dal), 79
  Lentil Loaf, 92
  Lentil Spaghetti Sauce, 86
  Quinoa Pilaf, 83
  Roasted Vegetables, 81
  Roasted Winter Squash, 81
  Roasted Yam Fajitas, 87
  Spaghetti Squash au Gratin, 80
  Sweet and Sour Tofu, 88
  Tofu Lasagna, 89
  Tortilla Bean Pie, 90
  Vegetarian Quiche with Basmati
    Crust, 91
Milk:
  about 46
  Amazing Quiche, 46
  Bananarama Tofu Boost, 19
  Chocolate Banana Malt, 18
  Jake's Shake, 18
  Mocha Latte Smoothie, 17
  Peanut Butter Cup Smoothie, 18
  Pumpkin Pie Shake, 18
  Shake on the Run, 18
  Strawberry Banana Smoothie, 17
  Traditional Custard Sauce, 97
  Vegetarian Quiche with a Basmati
    Crust, 91

Mushrooms:
  Barley Mushroom Pilaf, 82
  Ground Beef Stroganoff, 27
  Quick Chili, 28
Nutritional supplements:
  about 110
Nuts:
  about 58, 103
  Broccoli Walnut Salad, 58
  Granola with a Crunch, 95
  Homemade Muesli, 21
  On-the-run Breakfast, 20
  Roasted Almonds, 103
  Salmon Waldorf Salad, 32
Onions:
  Garden Vegetable Casserole with
    Rice, 85
  Roasted Vegetables, 81
Oranges:
  Orange Carrot Soup, 53
  Tropical Cheesecake Smoothie, 19
  Tuna Citrus Spinach Salad, 33
Peanut Butter:
  about, 18
  Hummus, 39
  Peanut Butter Cup Smoothie, 18
  Peanut Butter Granola Bars, 100
  Thai Peanut Sauce, 38
Pears:
  Homemade Muesli, 21
  Indonesian Curried Salad, 25
Peppers:
  Garden Vegetable Casserole with
    Rice, 85
  Jiffy Grand Beef Stir-fry, 28
  Lettuce Wraps, 29
  Quinoa Pilaf, 83
  Roasted Vegetables, 81
  Turkey Cacciatore with Peppers, 26
Pineapple:
  Spicy Pineapple Chicken, 23
  Sweet and Sour Tofu, 88
  Tropical Cheesecake Smoothie, 19
Pita:
  Mediterranean Pita Pizza, 27
  wrap/pita combos, 34
Pizza:
  Curried Tuna Pizza, 31
  Mediterranean Pita Pizza, 27
  Thai Chicken Tortilla Pizza, 24

Poultry:
  Homemade Turkey Sausage Patties, 47
  Turkey Cacciatore with Peppers, 26
  Turkey Pesto Quesadilla, 25
  wrap/pita combos, 34
Protein:
  about, 26, 73
Pumpkin:
  Pumpkin Pie Shake, 18
Quick Prep:
  about, 12 – 15
  breakfasts, 20 – 21
  fish, 31 – 33
  ground meats, 27 – 30
  leftovers, 35 – 36
  meals, 23 – 36
  Mix and Match Wraps and Pitas, 34
  salsas, spreads and dips, 37 – 39
  shakes, 17 – 19
Quinoa:
  about, 83
  Quinoa and Black Bean Salad, 70
  Quinoa Pilaf, 83
Rice:
  about, 91
  Garden Vegetable Casserole with
    Rice, 85
  Lentil Rice Salad, 66
  Vegetarian Quiche with a Basmati
    Crust, 91
Salads:
  Asian Salad, 24
  Basic Coleslaw, 57
  Basic Salad, 55
  Big Batch Creamy Coleslaw, 62
  Broccoli Walnut Salad, 58
  Chicken Caesar Salad, 60
  Clean Sweep Salad, 36
  Colene's Spicy Carrot and Chickpea
    Salad, 69
  Colourful Black Bean and Corn Salad, 59
  Curried Chicken and Apple Salad, 63
  Greek Style Bulgur Salad, 71
  Indonesian Curried Salad, 25
  Kidney Bean, Cabbage and Feta
    Salad, 65
  Lentil Rice Salad, 66
  Mixed Bean Salad, 67
  Quinoa and Black Bean Salad, 70
  Salmon Salad Fajitas, 32
  Salmon Waldorf Salad, 32
  Tabouli, 68
  Taco Salad in a Tortilla Bowl, 29

Tangy Beet Salad Ring, 64
Tuna Citrus Spinach Salad, 33
Tuna Salad Mix, 31
Salsa:
  Big Batch Tomato Salsa, 37
  Black Bean Salsa, 37
  Fruit Salsa, 37
  Spicy Pineapple Chicken, 23
  Taco Salad in a Tortilla Bowl, 29
Sauces:
  Beef Stir-fry, sauce, 77
  Italian Tuna Sauce, 32
  Lentil Spaghetti Sauce, 86
  Light Tartar Sauce, 39
  Roasted Yam Fajitas, sauce, 87
  Sweet and Sour Sauce, 88
  Tzatziki Sauce, 38
  Thai Peanut Sauce, 38
  Tomato Spaghetti Sauce, 30
  Traditional Custard Sauce, 97
Shakes:
  Bananarama Tofu Boost, 19
  Chocolate Banana Malt, 18
  High Fiber Cleanse Shake, 17
  Jake's Shake, 18
  Lemon Tart Smoothie, 19
  Low-glycemic Shake, 17
  Mocha Latte Smoothie, 17
  Orange Creamsicle Shake, 17
  Peanut Butter Cup Smoothie, 18
  Shake on the Run, 18
  Strawberry Banana Smoothie, 17
  Sunrise High Energy Smoothie, 19
  Tropical Cheesecake Smoothie, 19
Snacks:
  about, 104
  Chickpea Snacks, 103
  Mini Pita Fruit Snack, 102
  Roasted Almonds, 103
  Tortilla Chips, 102
Soups:
  Black Bean Soup, 49
  Clean Sweep Soup, 35
  Creamy Roasted Vegetable Soup, 54
  Curried Sweet Potato and
    Cauliflower Soup, 54
  Hamburger Soup, 30
  Minestrone Soup, 48
  Orange Carrot Soup, 53
  Quick Chicken Soup, 23
  Red Lentil Soup, 50
  Split Pea Soup, 51

Spinach:
  Tuna Citrus Spinach Salad, 33
  Turkey Pesto Quesadilla, 25
  Fish Fillets on Spinach, 78
Squash:
  Creamy Roasted Vegetable Soup, 54
  Italian Tuna Sauce, 32
  Roasted Winter Squash, 81
  Spaghetti Squash au Gratin, 80
Stir-fry:
  Beef and Broccoli Stir-fry, 77
  Clean Sweep Stir-fry, 35
  Jiffy Ground Beef Stir-fry, 28
Strawberries:
  Lemon Tart Smoothie, 19
  Strawberry Banana Smoothie, 17
Sweet Potato:
  about, 87
  Curried Sweet Potato and
    Cauliflower Soup, 52
  Roasted Vegetables, 81
Tofu:
  about, 43, 88
  Bananarama Tofu Boost, 19
  Egg and Tofu Scramble, 43
  Sweet and Sour Tofu, 88
  Tofu Fruit Custard, 97
  Tofu Lasagna, 89
  wrap/pita combos, 34
Tomatoes:
  about, 86
  Big Batch Tomato Salsa, 37
  Garden Vegetable Casserole with
    Rice, 85
  Hamburger Soup, 30
  Italian Tuna Sauce, 32
  Lentil Spaghetti Sauce, 86
  Mediterranean Pita Pizza, 27
  Quick Chili, 28
  Tomato Spaghetti Sauce, 30
  Turkey Cacciatore with Peppers, 26
Tortilla(s):
  Bean Burritos, 44
  Curried Tuna Pizza, 31
  Egg Tortilla Bowls, 45
  Roasted Yam Fajitas, 87
  Taco Salad in a Tortilla Bowl, 29
  Thai Chicken Tortilla Pizza, 24
  Tortilla Bean Pie, 90
  Tortilla Chips, 102
  Turkey Pesto Quesadilla, 25
  wrap/pita combos, 34

Vegetables, Assorted (also see specific
    vegetables):
  about, 69
  Garden Vegetable Casserole with
    Rice, 85
  Lentil Loaf, 92
  "Old Fashioned" Hearty Beef Stew, 75
  Quinoa Pilaf, 83
  Roasted Vegetables, 81
  Roasted Yam Fajitas, 87
  Tofu Lasagna, 89
  Vegetarian Quiche with a Basmati
    Crust, 91
Walnuts:
  about, 58
  Apple Custard Crumble, 96
  Fiber Feast Bread, 101
  Granola with a Crunch, 95
  Hearty Oatmeal Pancakes, 42
  Homemade Muesli, 21
  Old Fashioned Oatmeal, 21
  Peanut Butter Granola Bars, 100
Yams:
  about, 87
  Roasted Yam Fajitas, 87
Yogurt:
  Dip with a Twist, 38
  Fruit Dip, 38
  Ground Beef Stroganoff, 27
  Homemade Muesli, 21
  Hummus, 39
  Lemon Tart Smoothie, 19
  Mint Yogurt Dip, 38
  Salmon Salad Fajitas, 32
  Salmon Waldorf Salad, 32
  Shake on the Run, 18
  Sunrise High Energy Smoothie, 19
  Tropical Cheesecake Smoothie, 19
  Tzatziki , 38
Youth:
  cardio vascular disease, 104
  nutrition, 23
Zucchini:
  about, 85
  Garden Vegetable Casserole with
    Rice, 85
  Quinoa Pilaf, 83

Acknowledgements

To our families and friends who gave of their time, energy and patience to make this project a reality, we offer our heartfelt appreciation. The success of *Low-Glycemic Meals in Minutes* is a result of team effort!

To Laura's family: Rob, Jake, Anya and Grandma Irene, and Cheryl's family: Noel, Aaron, Evan and her mother Colene, we thank you for all your support and patience while we worked the many hours needed to get the project done. A special thanks to Aaron who came home at lunch to test our creations and help us with our computer glitches.

Deepest appreciation to Kelly Pape, our food photographer who spent long hours shooting pictures, editing and food styling, but most of all for all the laughs we had in the process.

Hats off to Sheryl Giudici, R.D., who was instrumental with recipe testing, editing and nutrition review. Special thanks to Gaye Dunkley for compiling the index, to Goldie Preziosi for proof reading the final drafts, to Lisa McCauley for her creative input, to Teresa Meierhofer for her food styling flair, and to John Kinnear for his creative guidance with the cover shot.

A special thanks to our USANA Team Vitality for their ongoing support and encouragement, and particularly for all the fun times we shared at potlucks and socials enjoying our low-glycemic recipes. And yes, tofu lasagna does taste good.

Testing over 125 recipes was a big job and we thank our cookbook helpers and recipe testers: Joan Siebel, Gaye Dunkley, Sharon Smith, Celine Calfa, Hazel Bauer and Ashley Wan. We also extend our thanks to Sahali Safeway for creating a photo opportunity.

A bouquet of roses to the team at Wayside Press, especially Glenda Mathew, our graphic designer whose editorial and design expertise moved us along quickly.

And to our mentor, Ray D. Strand, M.D., for his guidance, inspiration and support to provide a practical tool that will assist people with the skills to make low-glycemic meal preparation easy: the healthy choice also needs to be the easy choice — and we thank Dr. Strand for paving the way with his educational books and resources.